LUCY CALKINS AND LEAH MERMELSTEIN

Launching the Writing Workshop

DEDICATION

To Carl Anderson, with appreciation for his respectful attention to quiet voices and small moments.

FirstHand
An imprint of Heinemann
A division of Reed Elsevier Inc.
361 Hanover Street
Portsmouth, NH 03801-3912
www.heinemann.com

Offices and agents throughout the world

WITHDRAWN

Copyright © 2003 by Lucy Calkins and Leah Mermelstein

All rights reserved. No part of this book may be reproduced in any form or by any electronic or mechanical means, including information storage and retrieval systems, without permission in writing from the publisher, except by a reviewer, who may quote brief passages in a review.

Photography: Peter Cunningham

Rubrics and checklists adapted by permission from *New Standards*. The *New Standards®* assessment system includes performance standards with performance descriptions, student work samples and commentaries, on-demand examinations, and a portfolio system. For more information, contact the National Center on Education and the Economy, 202-783-3668 or www.ncee.org.

Library of Congress Cataloging-in-Publication Data

Calkins, Lucy McCormick.
    Launching the writing workshop / Lucy Calkins and Leah Mermelstein.
    p. cm. — (Units of study for primary writing ; 1)
    ISBN 0-325-00533-8 (pbk. : alk. paper)
    1. English language-Composition and exercises-Study and teaching (Primary)—United States.   2. Curriculum
    planning-United States. I. Mermelstein, Leah. II. Title.
    LB1529.U5C354 2003   2003019530
    372.62'3--dc22

Printed in the United States of America on acid-free paper

07   06   05   ML   4   5

P9-CDX-962

SERIES COMPONENTS

▶ **The Nuts and Bolts of Teaching Writing** provides a comprehensive overview of the processes and structures of the primary writing workshop.

▶ You'll use **The Conferring Handbook** as you work with individual students to identify and address specific writing issues.

▶ The seven **Units of Study**, each covering approximately four weeks of instruction, give you the strategies, lesson plans, and tools you'll need to teach writing to your students in powerful, lasting ways. Presented sequentially, the Units take your children from oral and pictorial story telling, through emergent and into fluent writing.

▶ To support your writing program, the **Resources for Primary Writers CD-ROM** provides video and print resources. You'll find clips of the authors teaching some of the lessons, booklists, supplementary material, **reproducibles** and **overheads**.

Launching the Writing Workshop

LAUNCHING THE WRITING WORKSHOP

Authorship of the Series

In primary classrooms, children sometimes work collaboratively on a shared piece. Some call the activity "Share the Pen." The phrase aptly describes the process through which these books have emerged. Although the text reads as if one person gave a minilesson and another transcribed and reflected on it, the process was actually much more collaborative. Always, the co-authors and I began by thinking and learning and planning and drafting teaching ideas together. Then one (and usually several of us) tried out the teaching ideas, usually in many classrooms simultaneously. Based on what we learned, we revised the general ideas, made plans for the general route a unit might travel and tried these plans in yet more classrooms. Finally the transcripts of a few minilessons began to emerge. These were then passed between the co-author and I with the details of the minilessons and the precise words to use with children emerging as we took turns working on them. Then we'd reassess the overall plan and set to work on yet more minilessons. Each book had its own support-cast and its own evolution.

About the Series

This series is for people who learn best by simply getting started. We hope teachers will regard the series as a sort of demonstration-teaching, and find companionship and comfort in its classroom specificity. It begins with Monday morning, with the decisions, words and insights that some of the nation's most respected teachers of writing make when we step past philosophy (and the place where everything is possible because no decisions have been made yet) and put ourselves on the line. We describe the days and weeks of a yearlong writing curriculum. We write in minute-by-minute detail so you can envision the words we actually say and the actions we actually take when we work with tiny writers.

We hope that by sharing our words and our decisions in all their specificity, we help you feel at home enough with teaching writing that you gather your youngsters close, and begin. For a time, you will probably adopt and adapt words and ideas you find here; know that each of us learned that way as well.

Because we have taught within a research and teaching collaborative, the Teachers College Reading and Writing Project, we've each listened in on and adopted the teaching language of mentors and colleagues, and drawn strength from the details of each others' teaching. This book is for teachers who may not be lucky enough to have the same daily opportunities to peek in on the teaching of mentors. We hope our teaching ideas slide on like new jeans, to be worn and shaped by you over time in ways that make them comfortable, inviting, endlessly functional and uniquely yours.

The series is comprised of nine small books and a CD-ROM. The first book, *The Nuts and Bolts of Teaching Writing* will equip you to teach a productive, well-managed writing workshop, introduce you to the methods that underlie all writing instruction, and help you plan a yearlong curriculum in the teaching of writing. Then, each of the seven unit books will support four to six weeks of that yearlong curriculum, helping you plan goals, minilessons, and shares for that unit. *The Conferring Handbook* offers you support in your conferring in each unit, and the CD-ROM offers resources and reproducibles to support you throughout the year's writing workshop.

Using the Sessions

1. SESSIONS

Sessions Each unit of study is divided into approximately fifteen teaching sessions; some sessions last a day; others need to be followed up with more minilessons in response to our children's needs and may involve two or three days. The session title identifies the topic of study.

Getting Ready The details of teaching matter. We list needed materials for each session.

The Introduction All teaching begins with research and deliberation. Here we share the thinking that led us to decide upon the particular emphasis for the day. In this way, we uncover the rationale for our decisions and reveal the beliefs that guide the day-to-day work we do with children.

2. THE MINILESSONS

We provide a ten-minute long minilesson that enables you to listen in on our actual teaching language and our children's responses. Each minilesson is divided into four components:

Connection: children access prior knowledge and hear the teaching point

Teaching: instructional language of the actual lesson

Active Engagement: children try or discuss what they've just been taught.

Link: we situate what we've taught into the larger context of all they've been doing.

These teaching moments are described both in concise statements in bold font, and in longer descriptions that capture the language and dynamics of real classrooms.

Commentary Alongside the teaching moments is your in-the-classroom literacy coach throughout the Unit of Study. In these comments, as in the introduction to each session and in other recurring sections throughout, we add more theory and professional advice to the teaching we have presented in the lessons.

3. TIME TO CONFER

As a unit of study progresses, the support you'll need to provide in one-on-one conferences is predictable. In this section, we set you up for success with one-to-one conferences, whispering key reminders to you as you head off to teach in response to what your children do and say and referring you to two additional resources for conferring. In your Units of Study package you will find a separate book titled *The Conferring Handbook*. Available separately is *Conferring with Primary Writers*, a larger guide to writing conferences. On this page we refer you to the specific conferences in both books that are most applicable at this point in the unit.

4. AFTER-THE-WORKSHOP SHARE

Every workshop ends with a reflective sharing session. After the Workshop Share helps you elicit reflections from students, or push them further, as they gather to talk about their work.

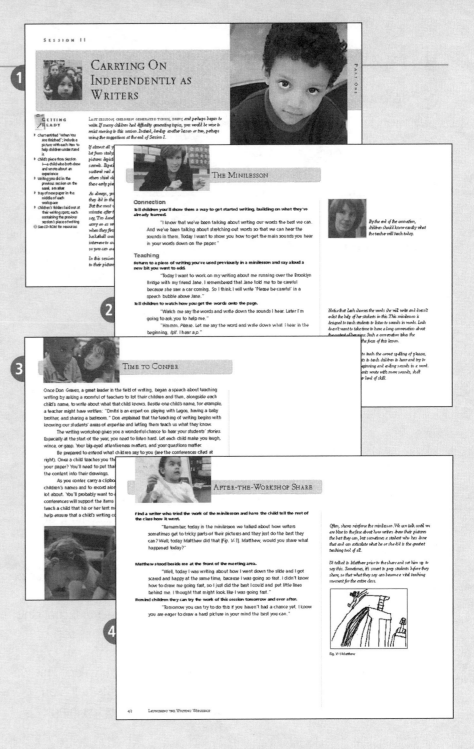

5 IF CHILDREN NEED MORE TIME

If children appear to need more time on the minilesson concepts, we often provide a list of the ways in which a teacher could develop several more minilessons patterned after (or based upon) the one we showcase.

6 ASSESSMENT

Assessment is woven throughout every aspect and moment of writing instruction. The assessment sections provide guidelines for understanding, monitoring and documenting what student writers have accomplished and where they are headed next so that we can adjust our teaching and curriculum in ways that respond to their unique needs and interests.

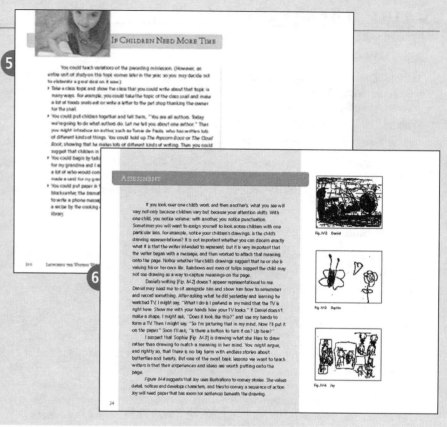

Each unit is divided into approximately fifteen sessions. In each session, we provide a detailed description of one day's teaching, and share ways in which that one day could be extended into several days.

This series grows out of the work that the Teachers College Reading and Writing Project does as staff developers in classrooms across the nation. We've found that some of the most powerful staff development occurs when we teach alongside other teachers, coaching into the nitty-gritty details of teaching. I've tried to bring this sort of coaching into this book. Often in the midst of a minilesson transcript, readers will find the words, "Notice especially the way . . ." or "This was a crucial move because. . . ." I hope that these comments help you glean larger principles from the fast-paced details of this teaching.

Why This Unit?

This book is for September. It is based on the premise that at the start of school, we mustn't waste a minute before issuing a broad and generous invitation to be sure each child feels at home in the world of written language. If children begin school by seeing themselves as the kind of people for whom the code of written language matters, they will be eager learners, taking in all they see.

Recently, I helped my three-year-old nephew slide each finger into the proper slot in his winter gloves. As I gave a final push to the last glove, Hugh pointed to the brand name label prominently displayed along the bottom of his glove. Running his finger slowly across each of the letters, he said, "That says *baseball glove*," and he gave me his melting smile. An hour later, Hugh was back, this time needing help removing the very same layers we had added earlier. As we worked, he confided, "I'm gonna make my cousin a police ticket. He was speeding." When Miles came in from the slopes, Hugh's efforts with marker pen and paper were underway. One glance told Miles that he could be in for some serious trouble with the local law, and soon he was on his knees beseeching the delighted three-year-old for mercy.

Hugh is growing up immersed in literacy. Even though he is only three years old, he is already a member of what Frank Smith refers to as the literacy club. He is an insider in the world of reading and writing, interacting with print for his own important purposes. Too many five- and six-year-olds watch people read and write and think, "That stuff is for someone else. I'm not even close to being the kind of person who can read and write," and so they mentally stand back from reading and writing. If a child has decided that writing is for other kids, not for him, then the child can be immersed in demonstrations of writing that barely enter his consciousness. The issue of identity, then, has everything to do with engagement.

In a similar way, it is easy for some teachers to read and hear about writing workshops, and to think, "Never, not in a million years of learning, could I teach that way." Leah Mermelstein, a colleague at the Teachers College Reading and Writing Project, and I have worked together to co-author this book on *Launching the Writing Workshop* because we believe that teaching writing shouldn't feel off-putting. We hope to provide the detailed and practical guidance that will help you feel as if you can approach the teaching of writing with the same verve and delight with which my nephew Hugh approaches literacy.

About the Unit

To an observer it will seem magical that by late September in a primary writing workshop, a teacher can convene her class on the carpet for a minilesson by simply saying, "Let's gather," or "It's time for writing," and within a few minutes children will have gathered around the teacher in an orderly cluster. It will seem magical that the teacher says, "Eyes, please," and children all (well, all but one or two!) look at her. Most of all, it will

seem magical that teachers send children off to draw and write, and lo and behold, the miracle happens. Children take their pens or markers, and they put themselves onto the page. They draw turtles and tall buildings, they make writing-like squiggles, alphabet letters that float across the page, or words that pin stories onto paper. Some sign their names; others label their drawings; some record long stories. No matter what they do, our children put themselves onto the page. The writing workshop is off and running. The important thing to know is this: none of this happens as a result of magic.

In September, we induct children into the structures and expectations of a writing workshop so that even in its opening days, children carry on with independence, making decisions without a teacher micro-managing their every step. This is only possible if the work is accessible enough for all children to do it easily and happily. The trick is to start the year with low expectations for the amount and quality of writing our students will do.

In early September, we have no alternative but to begin with what our children can do easily. We need to approach the first weeks of school determined that we will be perfectly happy if, at the end of the first few days, the workshop is a well-managed place, full of children who work with independence and initiative, even if no one has yet done much actual writing! During the very first days of a writing workshop, then, it is important to avoid focusing on letters and sounds. Your teaching won't *prevent* children from writing conventionally, but it should lessen the pressure and allow every child to carry on, doing whatever they can do easily (even if this is only drawing). Then, once the workshop feels like it is humming, you can intervene and teach in ways that lift the level of your expectations and of your children's work.

Before this first unit of study we, as teachers, need to be able to picture every detail of the writing workshop. We need to decide, for example, on the words or the signal to use to convene children in the meeting area. We need to imagine how our children will sit—perhaps cross-legged, shoulders facing forward, eyes towards us. We plan to explicitly teach these and other expectations. I know I'll give lessons on putting the cap back on markers, on taking just one marker at a time from the can, on moving quickly from the minilesson to one's writing spot. I know I'll need to follow-through on the routines I teach so that I turn words into practices, practices into habits.

Once children have begun to carry on independently and resourcefully, I don't hesitate to tell them that during writing time they must draw *and write.* There are educators whom I respect who do not share my belief that kindergarten children should be writing as well as drawing within a few weeks of the start of kindergarten. Usually these people will say that young children must begin the year with a focus on storytelling. I agree; in fact, this unit and the one that follows it are designed to help children sketch stories that span several pages and to tell and write these stories using story language. But, I also want children to have plenty of time to approximate working with print before they are expected to read and write conventionally. If a child has drawn a booklet full of pictures and told an accompanying story, it doesn't take anything away from the child's oral language work for that child to return to the picture and label *bike, me,* and *store* as best the child can. If the child hears only an *l-p* for *lollipop,* the effort to do this has still put the child into the place of wanting and needing to know letters—and this is a good thing. If the child hears the /b/ in *bike* and writes a squiggle in place of a letter, this is better than not stopping to hear the /b/. This means, then, that across the first unit of study, there will be changes in the work children do. Over time, children will begin to do more writing, and to write more conventionally.

STARTING THE WRITING WORKSHOP

GETTING READY

- Desks clustered to support the conversations
- Plans for your own short piece of writing, both important to you and true
- Chart paper, marker
- Stationery, an envelope, and some other kinds of texts (such as the words of a known song on chart paper)
- Paper for each child—for kindergartners, blank pages; for first graders, a space for drawing and a line or two for writing
- Marker or another writing utensil for each child, for after the minilesson
- Two-pocket folder for each child to store work in
- Way to take notes on your conferences—a notebook with a page for each child, in alphabetical order, might be helpful
- See CD-ROM for resources

TO LAUNCH THIS UNIT AND THE YEARLONG WRITING WORKSHOP, *we will demonstrate writing. Our goal is to offer children the opportunity to bring their lives to school and to put their lives on the page. At first, we're especially cultivating rich conversations, lots of storytelling, and detailed drawings. We definitely don't want children to limit what they say and think because of a concern for spelling or penmanship. We want to teach all children that the writing workshop is an opportunity to make and convey meaning.*

We'll start by demonstrating the whole act of writing and by inviting children to do likewise. We don't begin by breaking the process of writing down and asking children to do just one small part of that process. We believe it helps learners to have an image of the whole thing they'll be trying to do, even though it can feel ambitious to show them the whole thing and say, "Get started doing this." We know all children won't be able to do all of what we do on this, the first day of the writing workshop, but we want to give them the whole picture of what writers do.

By giving children a wide-open invitation into the whole act of writing, we also give ourselves a chance to see how much they can do without prejudging that they are ready only for one small step. Later we will slow down and show them aspects of the writing process that we trust will be especially accessible to them.

In this session, we will model the process of choosing a topic, sketching it, and then writing a tiny bit about it.

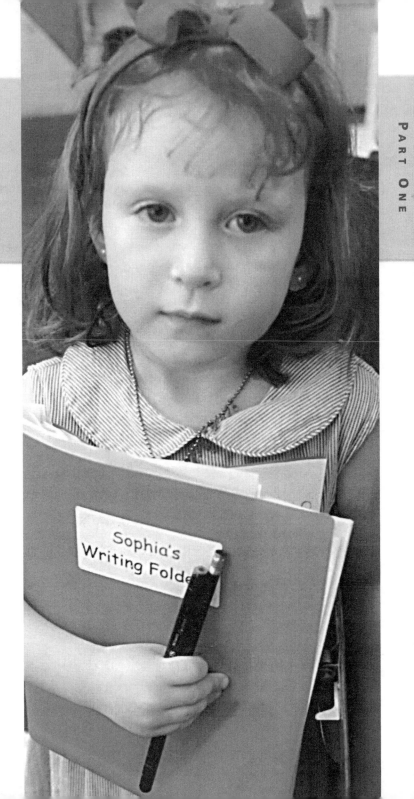

THE MINILESSON

Connection

Explain that every day children will work in a writing workshop and that the workshop will always begin with a meeting. Tell the children they are going to become writers.

"Writers, today we are starting something very exciting in our classroom called writing workshop. Every day at the start of writing workshop we will gather right here for a little meeting. We gather here because this is the most special place in the room." Leah gestured to all the beautiful books on the library shelves surrounding them. "We're wrapped in books. Every one of those books was written by an author, and this year you will all be authors too."

"We are going to write books like these," Leah held up a book, "and we will write songs like the ones we have been singing in our class," she gestured toward the words of a song, "and we will write letters." Leah held up stationery and an envelope.

"Today we are all going to be authors, and I will show you what authors do." Leah said this with a happy smile and an excited, confident tone.

Your confidence and enthusiasm will carry most of your children along. No matter how tentative and insecure you may feel, role-play your way into being confident of yourself and your children because they will hitch a ride on your enthusiasm.

The "visual aids" help more than you may realize—but only if you have the stuff on hand.

It's scary to begin. But across the nation, thousands of teachers bravely send children off to draw and write, and, lo and behold, the miracle happens. Children draw squiggles and turtles and tall buildings, they make writing-like graphics or alphabet letters that float across the page, and some record long stories. No matter what they do, children put themselves onto the page.

Teaching

Show children how you go about choosing a topic you know and care about.

"Watch what I do when I write." Taking hold of a marker pen, Leah cocked her head, pretending to search her memories.

"Hmmm. What should I write about?" Pausing, she said, in an unenthusiastic voice, "I could write about rainbows. . . . " Shaking her head as if to dismiss that very bad idea, she said, "But you know what, I never did anything with a rainbow! I want to write about what I do and what I know. Hmmmm."

"I know! I go running every morning, and funny things happen to me when I'm running. I can tell about what happened one day on my jog."

Show children that you begin by thinking about your subject, and then you sketch it from the image in your mind.

Leah looked at the marker pen in her hand. "Let me draw my story. Hmmm." Again Leah looked up pensively, she was remembering one time when she was running. Then Leah started to make a quick sketch. As she drew, she said, "Yesterday I ran across the Brooklyn Bridge. I splashed in a puddle and got mud all over my legs, so I am drawing about that time."

Leah made a drawing of the bridge, puddle, mud, and herself. While still intent on the quick sketching, she said, "Now I'll write my words."

Next, show children that you say the whole idea that you'll write, then you separate one word, or one part of a word, and then record it.

Looking at the picture, Leah said, "That's me so I'll write *me*." Then she said, "*Me, me, /m/*" and wrote an *m*. She repeated, "*me, me*" and completed the spelling.

"That's the bridge so I'll write *bridge*." Then Leah said, "*Bridge, bridge*, it starts like this," and she wrote a *b* beside the bridge in her picture.

Notice how Leah thinks aloud, highlighting the kind of thinking that she hopes her students will do.

Some children will be apt to select topics they can draw—like rainbows—so Leah anticipates and tries to avoid a predictable problem.

You won't want to use Leah's topic. Find one from your life. A story about a day when your dog ran away would be better than a story about your trip abroad since the latter would be broad and removed from most students' experiences. You'll work with the story you choose again in later minilessons. It should be about an ordinary and small event, chronologically ordered, bare-bones, and brief.

Notice that Leah chooses a story that is short enough to tell, draw, and write in just a couple of minutes.

Leah knows many of her children may not know enough about graphophonics, the way letters and sounds work, to be able to do as she does, but she doesn't withhold from them the fact that writers draw and then write. She wants all her children to do the same, and she expects them to write as best they can. She knows some will end up making letter-like squiggles, but this doesn't stop her from modeling how a writer listens to a word and records the sounds.

Then turning to the line under the drawing, Leah began to write her story. "I ran on the bridge," she said, then repeated, *I* and wrote it. This continued until she'd quickly written, "I ran on the bridge. I got muddy."

Tell children what you hope they saw you doing as you wrote and drew.

Turning now to talk to the children, Leah said, "Did you see what I just did? Did you notice that I first thought about something I did—running—and got it in my head? (At first I thought I could write about rainbows, but then I realized I never did anything with rainbows!) Did you notice how I thought about the times when I run in the morning, and I smiled because I love to run, and I remembered one recent time when I was running?"

Explain to the students that what you've demonstrated is what they will now do.

"I'm telling you about this because today (and every day) you can do the very same thing. You can think about things from *your* life, and you can write about them. I wrote about how I splashed in a puddle when I was running and you are probably not going to write about *that*, but you will think of something you do, something that has happened in your life recently. It could be something small, like maybe today when you were getting ready for school you lost your shoe. Or maybe your baby brother likes you to pretend you are a horse. Or maybe your baby sister spit up on you. Or you watched a driller blasting up chunks of pavement. Or your mother forgot to put the jelly on your peanut

This is sort of story Leah and I would use with New York City kindergarten, as well as first-grade, children. If you are concerned that this model is well beyond what your own kindergarten children can possibly do, continue to tell the rich story you tell, but—if you'd feel better doing so—write only labels and not sentences.

You are demonstrating the whole process of writing, but each child will attend to only the parts of this demonstration that he or she can use. Some children will take in only the fact that you drew something and made little marks called "writing" here and there. Only some will pay attention to the print at the bottom of the page. If you break this into steps and do a lot of explaining, your minilesson will become too ponderous to be effective, and it will cease being a model. Trust in the power of demonstration.

Notice that Leah asks rhetorical questions and answers them herself. She does not invite the children to answer at this point because she wants to keep her lesson short and focused. She will encourage children to participate in the next section of the minilesson.

Notice that Leah suggests two or three possible topics, each a very ordinary everyday occurrence. With all these examples in the air, it is less likely every child will decide on a running story!

Early in the passage above, Leah says a phrase that you will want to borrow verbatim. "I'm telling you this because today and every day you can do the very same thing." This can become like a mantra in your classroom for this minilesson and for the rest of your minilessons to come.

butter and jelly sandwich. If your life holds adventures like these, you definitely have stories to tell. These are all wonderful topics for writing. You can write about any little thing that happens in your life."

Active Engagement

Ask children to think of a topic they'll write about and to tell someone that topic.

"Can you close your eyes right now and think of something from your life that you could draw and write about?" After a moment's pause, Leah said, "Would you open your eyes and tell someone what you might write about today?" For a few moments, the room echoed with chatter.

Link

Ask children to begin writing on their own.

"Wow!" Leah said over the din as a way to say, "May I have your attention? May I have your eyes up here?" she whispered, as always waiting until the children seemed ready to listen.

"Writers, when I call on you, would you come up and get your writing paper and your writer's marker, and then you can go back to your desk and get started doing what writers do. I'll come around to admire the good work you are doing."

Eventually you'll have children in partnerships and you'll be able to say, "Tell your partner," but like many structures, you haven't set up partnerships yet. For now you just say, "Tell someone what you might write about," and you know that if your children have never experienced this ritual, some will sit there gaping, unclear why the room has erupted with noise. Crouch low and talk to a child or two, and get them talking to each other. Before long children will know what's expected and use this time well.

After two minutes, you will need a signal to help them get quiet again. The transitions will get easier as children become more accustomed to this structure.

For now, to minimize chaos, Leah doles out the materials and keeps them very simple—one page, one marker. She will dole out the materials for the first few days of writing workshop.

TIME TO CONFER

Today, your children will probably be able to write for twenty-five or thirty minutes. During that time, you'll want to conduct brief and, most important, warmly supportive conferences with six or seven writers. Plan to move all over the room. You'll probably want to carry a tiny chair with you so you can slip in alongside writers, sitting at eye level with them.

▶ Begin by asking the writer, "What have you been working on?" and "Will you read it to me?" Do this even if the "story" appears to be a scribble. If the writer can't recall, shift and ask, "What do you want to put down on paper?" or "What would you like your writing to say?"

▶ As soon as you hear the writer's message, whether it was written or not, respond with interest to the content. For now, your writing conference will sound very much like the conversation you have at the start of the day, when children come to you with their news and treasures. The only difference is that after showing interest, you'll also say, "You should put that on the page!" For now, it doesn't matter if the child draws or writes the content.

▶ You can find a model for the conference you'll have today by looking in *The Conferring Handbook* (see first conference at right). Try to notice the rhythm, the flow of that conference, and to let your conference follow similar patterns. It will help you and your children if you move to more ambitious conferences only after becoming accustomed to the components of conferring you see in Zoë's work with Bryanna. Notice especially the way Zoë tries to teach this child about what writers often do.

This conference in *The Conferring Handbook* may be especially helpful today:

▶ *"What's the Story in This Picture?"*

Also, if you have *Conferring with Primary Writers*, you may want to refer to the conferences in part one.

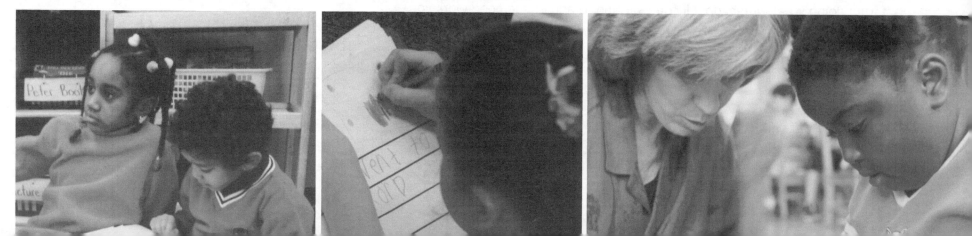

AFTER-THE-WORKSHOP SHARE

End the children's work time, ask them to put their work away, and gather them to share their work.

"Writers, will you put your writing into the folder that I've just put next to you? That is your writing folder." Leah held a folder and a piece of writing up to illustrate. "Then will you join us, folders in hand, on the rug? *Every day* after you have time to write, you'll put your writing in your folder," Leah demonstrated as she spoke, "and every day you'll come join us on the rug."

Ask children to share their work by holding it up for the world to see.

"How many of you put something on the page?" Leah asked. "Great! When I point to you, hold your writing up high so we can all admire it." Leah next acted like a conductor, with children proudly hoisting pictures and writing overhead.

Point out what you hope they will do in their writing—include details, depict a small, important moment, write words, and do more you admire.

"Writers, would you all admire what Liam did. Liam, show the class your work [*Fig. I-1*]. Do you see that Liam put details in his picture! He has himself," Leah pointed to herself, "and a flower because he was in a garden, and a sun." Leah pointed to the sun. "Liam told me his story and it goes, 'One day I went to the park with my Dad. We saw flowers. It was sunny.' Liam—are you going to add your dad? Because I don't see him on the page." Liam nodded.

Our workshops are brief during the first week. It won't be long before we ask for the class's attention. Just before we do this, we will pass out two-pocket folders, one to each child.

The folders are a way to set children up to work on pieces for more than one day, and to not necessarily progress in sync with each other, starting and stopping work on particular pieces at the same time. In later sessions, we'll encourage children to work on pieces for more than one day and we'll remind them to store their work in folders.

On this day, the share session will need to feel especially celebratory to set the tone for the year of writing workshop.

Fig. I-1   Liam

"Writers, would you admire Mikey's work too—Mikey, hold your story up [*Fig. I-2*]. Mikey has written some words (do you see them?) and they say, 'Me (and my) Mom (were) fixing . . .' and soon he's going to tell us what they were fixing. The lines in the story are rain because Mikey and his Mom were sitting under the trees (see that in the picture?) and it started to rain!"

"Mathew did something very special [*Fig. I-3*]. He made his brother (see, it says *B* for brother) and he decided to make his brother talking. Have you ever seen in comic books, how they have speech bubbles and each bubble contains the words someone says? That's just what Matt did. His brother is saying, 'Want to go to the beach?' and I bet tomorrow, Matt will tell us what his brother answers."

"Emma wrote a story that has two pages. She put a picture of a Mommy duck here, and a baby duck, and wrote words that went with the pictures. She wrote this." [*Fig. I-4*]

"I can't wait to learn what happens next, can you?"

End the writing workshop time with an exclamation of excitement for the writing to come and the start the children have made.

"Wow, look at all you've done! I'm so excited and interested to see what you all will choose to write about next!"

Fig. I-2   Mikey
Me and my mom were fixing...

Fig. I-3   Mathew

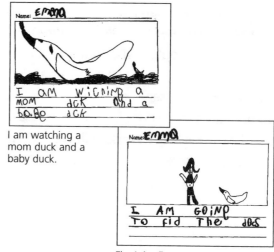

I am watching a
mom duck and a
baby duck.

Fig. I-4   Emma
I am going to feed the ducks.

IF CHILDREN NEED MORE TIME

We call each component in this book a session, not a day, because we know that fairly often you'll devote two days to one session. There are lots of ways you could devise a second minilesson to reinforce today's points.

▸ Instead of demonstrating your own writing process, you could demonstrate how a child in the class wrote. For example, you could say, "Jonathan started like this. He thought, 'Hmm. What should I write about?'" You can add in the story of his thinking. "He thought, 'I could write about battles, but I've never really been in one.'" After a few minutes of reenacting what Jonathan did the day before, get all the writers to imagine what they'll write about that day. "Writers, put on your thinking caps. What will you draw and write today?" Allow for a moment of silence. It is important for children to approach the page with a topic in mind rather than drawing whatever they can draw and then improvising a written text to accompany the art.

▸ Your minilesson might start, "Writers, I noticed yesterday that some of you sat down and thought, 'Hmmm—what can *I draw*?' and pretty soon you had a paper with flowers and rainbows. Today I want to teach you something. Writers don't start by drawing, we start *by thinking*. We *remember* things we've done. Watch. 'Hmm. I think I'll write about my sister's birthday party. I remember she had a huge cake. Let's see, I can remember the cake—it was flat. . . .'" Now you'd shift out of the role and list aloud the process: "Think first, picture it, then put it on the page. Right now, writers, will you think of something that happened to you, that you know about. Do you have the idea? Now picture it. Put a quiet 'thumbs up' if you are ready."

The writing workshop provides us with an amazing window into our children's understandings of written language. After even just one day in the writing workshop, we can bring our children's writing home and pore over it. Each piece of writing helps us develop a theory of the writer and his or her knowledge of literacy.

Margay, for example, relies on a few high-frequency words [*Fig. I-5*]. I will be interested to see if this is a pattern. I'm interested that she has fearlessly tackled words such as *read*, *draw*, and *spell*, representing each sound (including the vowels) with a letter. She seems able to invent spellings but may be hesitant to do so. I notice that her text is brief for someone with her skills. What would her writing have been like if she did it on lined paper? I plan to nudge her to write more.

When Ryan colored in his whole picture space [*Fig. I-6*], was he trying to represent nighttime? On the lines, he copied the alphabet. I wonder what he thinks he has done. I long to ask, "What's your writing about?" or "Will you read me your writing?" and to learn whether he believes his print carries meaning.

I plan to suggest we write something together and then elicit some content from him. Then I'll ask him to write the first word and I'll learn more about this mystery.

Sebastian's drawing seems to contain a whole drama [*Fig. I-7*]. I don't know if this is one guy who's gotten into lots of predicaments or if it's a flock of guys. I wonder what Sebastian will do when I ask, "Will you read me your writing?" I wonder if he thinks he has written a story, or if he regards this as only the illustration and plans to write a text.

Fig. I-5   Margay
I can write.
I can read.
I can spell.
I can draw.
I can do math.

Fig. I-6   Ryan

Fig. I-7   Sebastian

CARRYING ON INDEPENDENTLY AS WRITERS

GETTING READY

- Chart entitled "When You Are Finished"; include a picture with each item to help children understand it
- Child's piece from Session I—a child who both drew and wrote about an experience
- Writing you did in the previous session on the easel, a marker
- Tray of new paper in the middle of each workspace
- Children's folders laid out at their writing spots, each containing the previous session's piece of writing
- See CD-ROM for resources

LAST SESSION, CHILDREN GENERATED TOPICS, DREW, *and perhaps began to write. If many children had difficulty generating topics, you would be wise to resist moving to this session. Instead, develop another lesson or two, perhaps using the suggestions at the end of Session I.*

If almost all your children generated topics and texts, you will have learned a lot from studying their work. You probably found that some drew detailed pictures depicting true-to-life scenes, and others drew floating images or scrawls. Especially if these are first graders, some wrote sentences, others scattered real and approximate letters throughout their pictures, and still others shied clear of letters altogether. What a treasure trove of information these early pieces are! Study them well and record your findings.

As always, you could spend more time helping children do better at what they did in the previous session—storytelling with more details, for example. But the most urgent issue raised in Session I was probably the fact that five minutes after the writing workshop began, children started popping up to say, "I'm done!" If so, the next step should be to create a context for children to carry on as writers. Your goal is to help writers continue working beyond when they first consider themselves finished, so you can confer. Just as a basketball coach needs to first get the players playing and only then to intervene to coach individuals, so too you need to get the entire class working so you can coach individuals.

In this session you will show writers how to keep working by adding more to their picture or words or by starting a new piece.

The Minilesson

Connection

Remind children that today and every day the writing workshop will begin with a minilesson. Remind them of what happens in a minilesson.

"Writers, I'm glad to see you all sitting on your bottoms, thank you, and sitting on your rug spots, ready for our minilesson. Today and every day, we'll start the writing workshop with a minilesson. In a minilesson, I first remind you of what we've been doing and then I will tell you what we'll learn today. Then I will always teach—I will show you something you can do. During that first part of the minilesson, your job is to listen and to learn. You don't talk much during that part. Then after I teach you something, we all try it on the rug. After that, I'll send you off to work on your writing and I'll remind you that you might want to do what we learned about today or on an earlier day."

"Writers, yesterday you each did what real authors do. You thought of something in your life, got a picture in your mind, and then you drew and wrote about it. Ashley first thought about having macaroni and cheese for supper." Leah put her finger on her chin and looked skyward showing what Ashley may have looked like when she thought about the macaroni and cheese, "and then she drew herself and the bowl." Leah showed Ashley's picture while pointing to the word. "And then Ashley wrote, 'Yumm!'"

Professional development courses often teach teachers the architecture of a minilesson. Children also profit from having a sense for how minilessons generally go. In your overview of the components you will teach children what their roles are in different sections of a minilesson.

Leah does some smart things here. She refers to these children as authors. One of the most important things we can do is to make all our children feel like insiders in the club of authors. Then, too, Leah doesn't speak in generalities about the work these children did yesterday but instead uses the detailed retelling of one child's work to illustrate what every child did. In this way, her minilesson (like most good writing) uses detail to make a memorable point. Ashley's topic—eating macaroni and cheese—illustrates that writers can write about tiny, everyday moments, elevating these by turning them into literature. By retelling and reenacting what Ashley did the day before, Leah reminds her children that writers first think of their subjects and only then begin to record these on paper.

"You all did the same things—you thought, you drew, you wrote, and then," Leah's voice changed, "we had a problem. Do you know what it was? After you thought and drew and wrote, a lot of you came to me and said, 'I'm done.'"

Tell children what you'll teach them today: what writers do when they think they're done.

"Writers have a saying, 'When you are done, you've just begun.' Today I'm going to teach you what I do, and writers do, when we're done."

Teaching

Reenact the process of writing yesterday's story, showing children that when you are done, you decide to add on—to the writing, to the picture, or to a new story.

"Remember yesterday's story? Pretend it is yesterday and I am just now finishing my running story. Watch what I do when I am done with my writing." Leah turned to her writing and, looking intently at it, said to herself, "I got muddy" and wrote *muddy* again on top of yesterday's text. Leah looked up, pulling back from the work. She shook out her hand as if her fingers are ready for a break. "There, I'm done," she muttered in a voice loud enough for all to hear.

"Now watch." Leah drew herself back towards the page, looked intently at her picture. "I should add the tall buildings because they were all around." She did this. "Oh, and—" and she drew another runner, "That's Jane, she runs with me." She labeled the runner with the name *Jane*. "Now I think I will get another paper because this is giving me an idea for another story. I am going to tell about when Jane and I had a spaghetti supper together."

You can be a bit dramatic. As you present the scenario, all was going well yesterday. The children were all thinking, drawing, writing, and then—oh no—horrors! A problem: "A lot of children said, 'I'm done.'" This should strike home because most of your writers will have encountered what you are now calling a problem—the moment when they said, "I'm done."

Notice that this clean, precise, trim language helps teach young children. This is especially important now, at the start of the year. Your minilessons need to be simple, speedy, and clear. Your language will have more power if it is memorable. Use repetition, parallel construction, and active verbs to speak in memorable, forceful ways.

Notice that Leah demonstrates—or reenacts—rather than explains. Notice also that she returns to yesterday's story. Often the writing you use in a minilesson will thread through a dozen minilessons. Each time the text resurfaces, use it to make a new point. This works well because children come to know the text so well that their entire focus can be on only the new element of the text. This also helps get the idea of revision in children's minds long before you mention it to them.

Name what you've done that you hope your children will do now and always: Add to the picture, add to the words, or start new writing.

"Do you see what writers do when we are done?" Leah asked as she revealed a chart on the easel called "When I'm Done" with three items that Leah read aloud.

WHEN I'M DONE

* Add to the picture
* Add to the words
* Start a new piece

"Add to the picture like I did when I made the buildings and my friend." Leah sketched buildings beside the first item on the chart as a visual reminder.

"Add to the words like I did when I wrote my friend's name." Leah wrote *Jane* as the icon to accompany the second item from the list.

"Start a new piece like I did when I got a new piece of paper." Leah drew an empty piece of paper.

Active Engagement

Ask your students to imagine finishing, and then pulling back to their writing to add on or start new writing.

"Writers, I want you to close your eyes and imagine you are just finishing *your* writing." She paused so the children are with her. "You pull back," Leah acted this out, "and think, 'There, I am done. Whew. Done.'"

"But then you remember this minilesson and you imagine yourself pulling in again, close to the page." Again, Leah acted this out. She added, "and looking at your writing and thinking, 'Can I add more? Can I add more to my picture? To my words? Or should I go get more paper and start another?'"

Notice that Leah did not make the chart during the minilesson. She had the chart ready. She is conscious of time and keeps the lesson brief and lively. Notice also that when suggesting what children can do when they are done writing, none of the options are "play blocks" or "look at books." Writing is the only option during writing time. Leah wants to help children develop the stamina to write longer each day than the day before.

Leah finished the drama, "If you decide you need to get more paper, there will be more paper in the special tray at the middle of your table. If you finish one story and you have already added to the picture," she gestured to this item on the chart "or to the words," she gestured, "then you can come up and get a new piece of paper and go back to your seat and get started on a new story."

Link

Teach your students that the minilesson applies to their independent writing work. For today, remind them what to do when they are "finished" writing.

"So today, none of you will need to come to me and say, 'I'm done' because when you are done, you will have just begun. I can't wait to see you following our new chart." Leah pointed to it.

"If you are at the red table, you can go back to your places and get started."

To the remaining group, Leah said, in a voice that is loud enough for everyone to hear, "Let's watch these writers and see if they zoom to their writing spots and get out their paper." The writers, of course, follow her instructions. "Let's see if they think of something important and then start to draw. Are they doing that? Oh, look, Arthur is! Eddie is!" Now Leah turned her eyes back to the group at her feet and sends off another batch of children. Again she helped the class watch and admire these children settle into the work of being writers.

Later you will have more complicated (and probably more successful) forms of active engagement, but for now you are trying to keep the minilesson streamlined, and you want to teach only a few new habits and rituals each day.

Speak with confidence but meanwhile keep in mind that this minilesson is very ambitious. It's unlikely that from today alone, children will have learned how to keep going on their own, to get new paper when they need it, to spend more than one day working in a piece—all of this is a tall order.

Notice the way the end folds back on the beginning of this minilesson. It is cohesive. Your job as a teacher is to design and deliver minilessons in ways that make lasting impressions. Reiterating an early charge like, "When you're done, you've just begun," helps. Remember that it helps to repeat phrases that you hope will become part of children's thinking.

This is a smart way for Leah to teach children how to manage themselves without spending a lot of time or effort on it. She is trusting the children to do a good job with going back to their seats and getting started, and she is giving them a chance to rise to the challenge of having all eyes on them as they do this table by table. She will tackle some management issues in subsequent lessons, but for now her most important work is to help children generate ideas and put them on the page.

TIME TO CONFER

Once Don Graves, a great leader in the field of writing, began a speech about teaching writing by asking a roomful of teachers to list their children and then, alongside each child's name, to write about what that child knows. Beside one child's name, for example, a teacher might have written: "Dmitri is an expert on playing with Legos, having a baby brother, and sharing a bedroom." Don explained that the teaching of writing begins with knowing our students' areas of expertise and letting them teach us what they know.

The writing workshop gives you a wonderful chance to hear your students' stories. Especially at the start of the year, you need to listen hard. Let each child make you laugh, wince, or gasp. Your big-eyed attentiveness matters, and your questions matter.

Be prepared to extend what children say to you (see the conferences cited at right). Once a child teaches you their content, you'll want to say, "Where is that on your paper? You'll need to put that here." For now, don't worry if some children add the content into their drawings.

As you confer, carry a clipboard with you. You may want to make a chart of your children's names and to record alongside each name what it is that the child knows a lot about. You'll probably want to also carry Unit One's checklist. For today, your conferences will support the items listed under genre and purpose. Record when you teach a child that his or her text must convey a story or information and when you help ensure that a child's writing conveys meaning.

These conferences in *The Conferring Handbook* may be especially helpful today:

- ▶ *"What's the Story in This Picture?"*
- ▶ *"Where Is Your Writing?"*

Also, if you have *Conferring with Primary Writers*, you may want to refer to the following conferences:

- ▶ "What's the Story in This Picture?" (all versions)
- ▶ "What's *Happening* in Your Piece?"

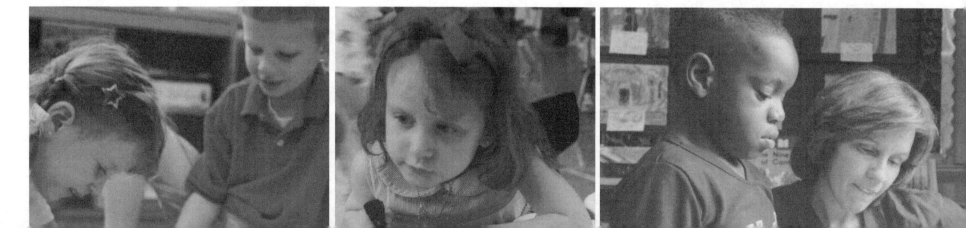

AFTER-THE-WORKSHOP SHARE

After you gather children together on the rug again, sum up what they have learned so far. You can do this by celebrating what they have done today.

"Writers, will you put your writing in your folder and bring it to the rug. I was so pleased to see that today, when I sent you off at the end of the minilesson, you went to your writing nooks like so," Leah reenacted a child moving quickly from the meeting to her desk place, "and got some paper from the pile in the middle of the table and wrote your name, and then you thought, 'What will my story be today?'" As she spoke, Leah did all this. "Soon you were putting your story on the paper!"

"And, I was pleased during writing time because I saw many of you finish a piece, and you pulled back and said, 'Whew! Done!' and then you said, 'Wait, I can probably do more,' and soon you were adding on to your writing," Leah motioned to the "When I'm Done" chart, "adding words or adding to your pictures. And finally, just now when I said, 'Let's gather,' I was pleased all over again at the end of writing time when you put your writing into your folders." Leah did this. "You are really getting the hang of how writing time works in our classroom. And I know that tomorrow and every day, you'll continue to do these things."

Notice that although this time is called a "share," it isn't necessarily a time to read aloud work. The share can serve almost as a second minilesson. You could, alternatively, have used this time to share. The share could have gone like one of these scenarios:

- *"When I point to you, will you stand up and tell all of us—using just one word—what you wrote about?"*
- *"Hold up your beautiful writing! Oh look, I notice that . . . and I notice that. . . ."*
- *"You know what I saw today? Some of you, like Joe, put lots of pictures on your paper and wrote about them. That's the same as Richard Scarry does in this book." You would hold up* What Do People Do All Day? *or another of his published books, open to a page in which he, too, has a bunch of pictures and some words near them. "And some of you, like Joline, made a story with no words at all but with pictures that tell a story. That's the same as Raymond Briggs did in this wordless book." You would again hold the text up, this time, Briggs' (The Snowman).*
- *"Wow! I learned so much about each of you today. I learned that Alex loves his family picnics because he wrote about it. Danielle loves to ice skate, and Sam is crazy about his dog. I know all these things because these writers wrote about them. From now on, we are going to live like writers who write about things they are very passionate about, that they are crazy about! Great writing, writers!"*

You could repeat a variation of this minilesson, but that's probably not necessary. It is more likely that you'll decide to develop a minilesson or two between this session and the next in which you teach toward a few other goals. The ideas listed below could become the content for minilessons, or they could become the content for a midworkshop teaching points or for future after-the-workshop shares.

▸ "Remember how we discussed things you could do 'When I'm Done'?" You refer to the chart. "It was great seeing many of you try some of the things on the list. I saw Jamie finish her work, pull back, and then think, 'Wait!' Soon she was adding trees and flowers to her story about riding the swings at the park. I saw Dorie add the word *mom* to her writing about her mom." You show Dorie's piece and gesture towards the appropriate item on the chart as you describe it. "That was so smart. Now, I want each of you to close your eyes and imagine getting out your old writing and thinking, 'Wait, I can do more to this.' Think how you could add to that writing. When you are ready, open your eyes. Maybe you can follow one of those plans today."

▸ "Marcus came to me and said, 'I want to start a new story, but I am not sure I am all done with my old writing.' Then he remembered that because he kept his old writing in his folder, he could go back to it anytime he wants. How smart! Because your old writing is right here in your folders, you can go back to it whenever you want."

▸ "Today, a friend of yours may forget our minilesson and come up to you to say, 'I'm done. What should I do?' Tell the person beside you what you could say."

▸ "Writers, I was looking at this book, *Good Night Moon*, and I saw that the author put her name on it. Same with this book. What if we agree, after this, that the first thing we, as writers, will do is put our names on our papers? Then we will draw."

USING SUPPLIES INDEPENDENTLY

GETTING READY

- Toolbox for each table, each containing cans of pencils and boxes of markers, plus a date stamp
- Writing folders, one for each child
- Boxes containing each table's worth of kids' folders, color-coded with stickers: a yellow sticker on the folders that belong in the yellow table's box, and so on
- Tray of new paper at each table
- See CD-ROM for resources

SINCE THE WRITING WORKSHOP BEGAN, YOU'VE BEGUN EACH WORKSHOP *by doling out the paper and the pens or markers. This has been the simplest way to expedite the work of the writing workshop—but it can't continue for very long because children need to have easy access to paper and markers whenever they need them, and you need to be free to teach.*

Some teachers, in an effort to maximize their teaching time, try to tuck management tips alongside their teaching, mentioning these tips as "by the ways" during minilessons that are focused on the writing process. We've learned over time that it is wiser to give management your full attention, devoting quite a few of your September minilessons to management issues.

Today, you'll move your students towards independence by teaching them where to find and how to take care of the tools they need for the writing workshop—cans of pencils, boxes of markers, the date stamp, and their writing folders.

THE MINILESSON

Connection

Tell children that writers not only write on topics they care about, but writers also have special writing tools.

"Writers, may I have your eyes please?" After a pause, I continued. "I am proud of all the work that you have been doing during writing workshop. Jose has been writing stories about the baseball games he plays, and Sarah has been writing about eating dinner at her Grandma's house."

"All of you have been writing about things that matter to you, just like writers do. Today I want to teach you one more thing that writers do. Writers have special writing tools—and we take care of them. Today I want to teach you how to get and take care of the supplies you need to write."

In these early minilessons, we are teaching children how to act during this important time. Insisting on children's eyes (and attention) is important.

Teachers sometimes think of paper and pens as school supplies, and we can take them for granted. But writers regard pens and paper as tools of our trade, and many of us care a great deal about these tools. By honoring them, we honor our craft. It's wise to help children value their writing tools, because as the year unfolds, they'll often receive new tools that represent (and lure children towards) new levels of work.

Teaching

Teach the students how the supply systems will work.

"Every writer needs a marker or a pen, and we need to have these close when we work so if we get an idea—we can just reach for a pen! On my desk, I keep this special jar for pens, so I always have one. Lots of grownup writers have these on their desks."

"In this class, you need to have pens close by, so we've got very special writer's toolboxes," I held one up, "and in them we have jars just like I have on my desk. We have a jar for pencils, and a jar for pens. We also have a date stamp because writers need to know when they wrote a piece—so we'll be dating our pieces every day." I demonstrated this.

"We'll also have a box for our folders. When it is time for writing, we will need table monitors to get the toolboxes and the folder crates out quickly, so no one wastes a precious moment of writing time."

Active Engagement

Demonstrate how the tools should be used, and have the children try a practice run.

"So let's pretend it's the end of writing time. I'll say, 'table monitors' and when I say that, then the six of you—your names are on the list, one for each table—will hop up like this, and come over here and get your tools." I acted out how they'll jump to their feet. "So let's try it, just to practice, okay? So writers, it's almost time to write. Table monitors, would you get the tools?" As six children jump up, I said to the remaining children, "Let's watch and see if they do this really quickly so we won't have to waste a minute of our precious writing time."

Notice the way managing supplies becomes another way to help children assume their identities as being writers. This makes sense. In life, we often do take on new tools to role-play our way into being the people we want to become. I buy a new jogging outfit in hopes that this will lure me to jog. These children need the tools of their trade—and they'll grow into the promise of those tools.

I emphasize efficiency for a reason. This way, we won't waste one precious moment of writing time. In this way, I elevate classroom management.

Link

Tell students this will be the daily system for using supplies in writing workshop.

"Writers, this is how we will always get the room ready for writing workshop. Now let's see if, when I call on you, you can go quickly from our meeting area to your writing spot. Those in the back can get started writing."

MID-WORKSHOP TEACHING POINT

Name the problem and show how it interferes with everyone's work.

"Writers, Celeste just told me she couldn't think because of the noise, and Dillon said *he* couldn't concentrate. I don't really think that's fair because they are writing really important stories and they can't do their best work. Would all of you use your two-inch voices, like this?" I spoke softly.

Point out how things feel and sound when things are going well.

After a few minutes of children working and talking softly, I said, "Writers, listen to how the room sounds. This is the sound of a good writing workshop."

Notice that I haven't told writers specifically what to do during today's workshop. My lesson has focused on one small aspect of the workshop only, but it hasn't set kids up for the work they'll do today. This is huge and important. Children are left to make choices and to use what I have taught on previous days to help them determine what they'll do today.

When I intervene to address the whole class, I always use the same signal to get their attention. After I say, "Writers," I wait until each child has stopped, and I wait until each child's eyes are on me. We practice this. Only then do I speak, and I speak softly.

TIME TO CONFER

During your conferring today, you'll want to follow the suggestions for Sessions I and II. Pay attention to children's drawings (see Assessment) and notice at least one more aspect of how each child works. Watch your children's abilities to be productive and attentive during writing time, and watch your abilities to discipline in ways that lift (rather than lower) everyone's spirits.

Resist the common tendency to begin conferring immediately. Instead, reserve three minutes at the start of writing workshop for "reading the room." Tell your children you're going to watch them carry on like writers. Tell them to try getting started without you. Explain that getting started is a grown up, "writerly" thing to do, and then watch. Don't fix every problem you see. Watch. Keep your unit checklist in hand. Children notice what you notice.

Notice your writers' use of tools and let children know you are watching this. Say loudly, "I'm watching and admiring the way this group of writers uses its writing tools. Oh! Look. Leo capped his markers!"

Notice the volume of sound. If it gets too loud, be prepared to intervene. You'll first need a way to get your children's attention (see the management chapter in *The Nuts and Bolts of Teaching Writing*). Teach this way to your children. Use it two to three times within the writing workshop.

Meanwhile, some of your conferences will be Expectation Conferences, designed to bring children into the norms of a writing workshop. Study the first section of "Where Is Your Writing?" in *The Conferring Handbook* and see the conferences cited at right in the *Conferring with Primary Writers* book. Be prepared to use similar language:

▶ I'm so surprised to see . . . writers don't . . . Do you think (Eric Carle) . . . No! Well, this is your time to write like (Eric Carle).

▶ You can . . . some other time. This is your precious writing time. So let's not waste one minute of it. . . .

▶ You know what a lot of writers need . . . I think you may be one of those writers who need. . . .

This conference in *The Conferring Handbook* may be especially helpful today:
▶ *"Where Is Your Writing?"*

Also, if you have *Conferring with Primary Writers*, you may want to refer to the following conferences:
▶ "Where Is Your Writing Work?"
▶ "Writers Share Community Supplies"

Go over the writing workshop routine with students.

"We've had a writing workshop for one week, and I'm wondering if you kids have realized how writing time always goes. There are things that we do every day. Count on your fingers with the person beside you, and see if you can list five things we always do in a writing workshop." The room erupted into conversation. After several minutes, I called for the children's attention and said, "Let's list what happens every day in a writing workshop."

- Every day we sit on our rug spots (we don't hover).
- Every day we put our supplies on our work places like we did today.
- Every day we bring folders to our tables.
- Every day we use the date stamp to date our papers.

Add one thing they still need to learn by citing a new writing supply-related task.

"Today I want to add one more thing."

- Every day we take care of our markers.

"We do this by snapping the markers shut. Listen." I snapped a cap onto a marker. "Did you hear the marker snap? When you are finished using a marker from now on, listen for the snap so that our markers will not dry out. Great work today!"

The ability to list parallel items that all pertain to a general category (such as "what happens every day in a writing workshop") is a skill that is foundational to nonfiction writing. It's helpful to teach children to think and talk in these ways long before we ask them to write in these ways.

Consider having some of these conversations during other subject areas throughout the day so as not to overburden writing time with management issues.

IF CHILDREN NEED MORE TIME

▸ Ask children to watch what you do as a writer, and then act out the wrong way to do things—shoving scrunched up paper into a folder, leaving open markers in the can, hoarding five markers. Then invite children to critique your behaviors. They'll laugh but they'll also learn.

▸ Turn the link—the final component—of any minilesson into an instructional opportunity. When you say, "Off you go," at the end of the minilesson, get the class to join you in watching a group of children do whatever it is you hope all children will do. Say "Let's watch as they go quickly to their seats, get their supplies, and get to work." While children do this, name what you notice they're doing to the rest of the class who'll still be at your feet. "Watch how the red table is walking straight to their writing nooks, not talking as they go to their nooks! See how each person got out his or her writing," and so on. "Which table of writers feels ready to do just as good a job as the red table? Okay blue table, let's see how you get started writing."

Remember that you cannot assess your children's abilities to hear and record sounds simply by looking at written products. Of course you'll notice whether this child or that one has made an effort to write with letters. But you will want to also coach or nudge the child to hear and record sounds. Only then can you make tentative assessments and plans based on them.

Coach	Notice	Assess & Plan
"Where are you in this picture? Oh. I see. So write *me*" (You point beside the picture).	Does the child say "me" to herself when nudged to write *me*?	If so, she's showing that she understands a writer says a word and then records it.
	Does the child isolate the /m/?	If so, she's well on her way to recording sounds. Isolating and hearing a distinct phoneme is half the battle.
	Does she say "'me' /m/ /m/" and record something entirely different?	If not, join her in isolating and attending to the first sound. "Watch me, watch my mouth. Say it with me. Do you hear the /m/ at the start of *me*?" You are coaching her in phonemic awareness. If she records something different, she will have done a lot that is right. She will have isolated the initial sound and recorded it with a letter. Keep watching. Don't stop her to correct it. Does she reread the letter? If so, does she act as if it says *m* or *me*? You could help her move on to the next label, or you could say, "Actually, this is how you write the letter that makes a /m/ sound," and then show her the letter.

TELLING STORIES IN ILLUSTRATIONS

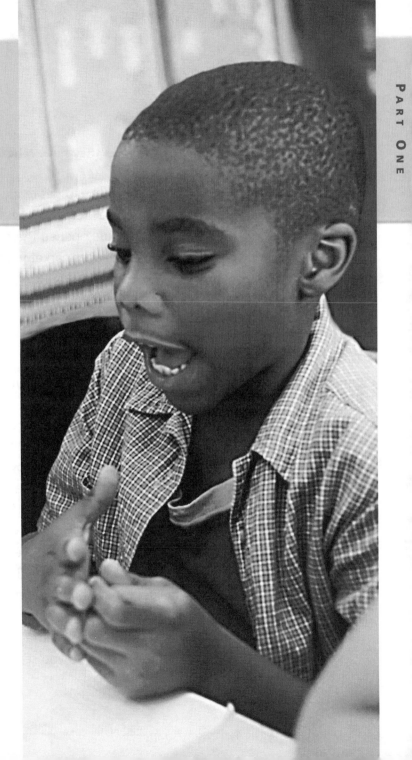

GETTING READY

- Chart paper, marker
- Tiny story to plan and write with students about something they've lived through as a class
- *My Little Island* by Frane Lessac, page 32, or a different detailed illustration; you may need copies or an overhead projector and transparency of the illustration so everyone can study it at once
- See CD-ROM for resources

PRIMARY STUDENTS OFTEN, IF LEFT TO THEIR OWN DEVICES, *begin writing workshop by drawing a picture. Then they create a story around that picture. That is, they draw a frog, and then decide to draw a lake, and finally invent a story about frogs jumping into lakes. Although there is no great harm in having a drawing dictate the content, there is a place for teaching students that writers usually plan what they will write and that writing workshop is an opportunity to convey important meanings. Today you will ask students to close their eyes and picture something that happened to them that they want to put onto their paper. The next task will be to encourage them to make drawings that are representational.*

This session will teach students that writers can decide on a topic, envision it, and then record that meaning on the page with drawings that are representational.

THE MINILESSON

Connection

Remind students about some of the ways they have rehearsed their writing before they've written.

"Writers, you know lots of ways to get ready to write. Sometimes you close your eyes and think of an idea. Yesterday when I was watching Jose write, I saw him close his eyes, and then he opened them and told me that he was going to write about going to the supermarket with his mother."

Tell students that you'll teach them to approach writing with an idea in mind.

"Today I want to teach all of you how to start with an idea for writing and to put that idea on the paper."

Teaching

Demonstrate this concept by telling a story about an event the class experienced. Draw the details you envision.

"Writers, today I'm going to do what Jose did, and what I hope all of you do. I'm going to close my eyes and get a story of something I've done in my head." Leah closed her eyes and dramatically showed that she is deep in thought. "Okay, I've got it. I'm going to write the story about yesterday when we found the snail during independent reading. Here is how it goes:"

"'Our class snail was missing. We were all worried. During independent reading, Andy found the snail in his book. We were glad.'"

"Okay, now I want to get the whole story in my illustrations. First I'll draw Andy and I'm going to make his mouth look worried because he was worried." Leah drew for a moment, then looked at what she'd drawn. "Ohh!" she added. "I better draw myself sitting with Doug because I was reading with him."

Leah turned back to the class. "Do you see how I'm putting the whole story into my picture?"

Remember that you are teaching children not only how to write but also how to be members of a writing workshop. Here Leah reminds children that each day's minilessons accumulate, and that consequently children are developing a repertoire of strategies.

Notice that Leah reenacts the step-by-step process she hopes her children will follow. She demonstrates rather than summarizing and explaining.

Active Engagement

Have the students join in to help you add parts of the story to the illustration.

"Will you all help me now? Turn to the person next to you and think about what other parts of the story I could put into the illustrations."

Leah bent down, listening and responding to what the students said. "I've listened to all your smart ideas and right now I'm just going to add two of them and perhaps later we'll add more. Cecilia thought I should add some of the children running over so I think I will, and Tony thought I should make my face look surprised because I kept saying, 'I can't believe it!'" Leah quickly added these two details to the illustration.

Link

Remind students to get a picture in their minds before they write, and then to add details they envision to their drawings. Get them started envisioning before they go off to write.

"So, today and every day as you write, make sure you picture what happened and then put the details of your story in your illustrations. Let's get ready to write. Close your eyes. Once you get the story in your head, open them and signal with a thumbs up that you're ready to write."

Remember, this is a story that the students know well. It was a shared experience; therefore, students won't need to search for details.

Leah was careful to ensure that this minilesson didn't turn into a maxilesson. She summed up what some of the students said, rather than having them share all their ideas. This is a smart technique to ensure brevity.

Notice that the students are taking a moment to plan before they write. Although the students are active, this is not part of the active engagement because the students are no longer practicing the minilesson, but rather are preparing to write.

TIME TO CONFER

As you add new conferences to your conferring repertoire, don't forget the ones you learned early on. Remember especially the early emphasis on listening attentively to the child's meaning. Most of the time, meaning will be conveyed by the child's pictures, so study them with care. Keep in mind that in a good conference, the child teaches you, and you listen in ways that help the child realize how much he or she has to say. We all have people in our lives who listen so responsively that they often get us to say more than we'd normally say. Be *that* kind of listener.

But in this conference, begin to keep in mind that this listening can be responsive and yet brief. Get used to the rhythm of listening for a minute, and then of letting your conference turn a bend towards the goal of getting each child to put his or her content on the page.

By now, you'll want to use conferences as a time to help children get some writing down on the page. It will help you enormously to read the Pathways chapter (in *The Nuts and Bolts of Teaching Writing*) and find a few categories of writers that describe your kids. Study the tiny details of how I suggest you teach these kids. For now, you may want to focus on children who represent two of those categories; for those children, try to follow my instructions carefully. It will help if you study a few conferences in which we support very early writing. See the conferences cited at right. If you are new to this, get a teacher-colleague to role-play a very little child while you role-play the teacher, so you have a chance to practice the moves.

These conferences in *The Conferring Handbook* may be especially helpful today:

- ▶ *"Where Is Your Writing?"*
- ▶ *"Let Me Show You How to Write More"*

Also, if you have *Conferring with Primary Writers*, you may want to refer to the following conference:

- ▶ "Can I Show You How to Write What Happened First, Then Next, Then Next?"

Ask children to study an illustration that contains enough details to tell a story in itself.

"Writers, I've made an overhead of one of the illustrations that the writer Frane Lessac used when she, like all of you, did a piece of writing." Leah held up *My Little Island*. "Would you and the person beside you really study this picture and see if you can figure out what's happening in it?"

"Like you kids, Frane wrote the story that goes with her picture. Her picture is about when she went back to the Caribbean island where she was born. Beside this picture, she wrote:

> [There] is a wild, wild forest where we go fishing. We don't want to scare the fish, so we stand there quietly and just listen to the birds' songs and frogs and insects and the sound of the bubbling mountain stream.

You can look in the picture and see all those things—the fish, the birds, the kids fishing, the stream. That's what writers do. We put our stories into our pictures and into our words."

Ask children to do the same kind of studying with their own pictures.

"Now, would you show the person beside you *your* picture? Study each other's pictures and tell the story of your picture just like you told the story of Frane Lessac's picture."

You'll want to use a predictable signal to convey to students that it's time to stop talking with partners and to focus on you again. Some teachers say "writers" and some start a soft hum.

Either way, students should be getting more and more used to turning to a partner, talking for a few moments, and then turning back to you. If students are having trouble making this move smoothly and quickly, you'll want to set aside the next session to help them practice doing this with ease. Talk is crucial in the writing workshop, and students need to be able to talk with one another easily without interrupting the flow of the minilesson.

Again and again throughout all workshop teaching, we will show the students the work of a published author or illustrator and help them learn what is going on within that work so that they can do the same.

As before, you'll want to give children enough time to notice and talk through a few things in the pictures, but not enough time to finish all they can easily say.

Suggest children could add details to their illustration. Show them an example.

"Thumbs up if you are realizing you *could* add more detail into your illustrations. Good! Let me show you another example. Notice the beautiful detail Ava put into her story. If you look closely, you'll see a line of people and one of the people seems to be drinking out of a bowl on the floor! Weird, right? But listen to Ava's story." [*Fig. IV-1*]

"I bet you can't wait to read Ava's story! The details in her illustrations really help. I bet you can't wait to get to writing again to work on more details!"

This move to show children another example, this time from a classmate's illustration, can help children see that published authors and children like them can both do the same work. This gives them confidence and helps them see themselves as writers.

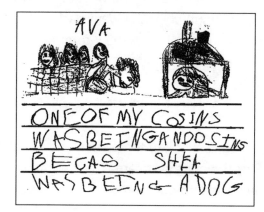

Fig. IV-1   Ava

One of my cousins was being a nuisance because she was being a dog.

If Children Need More Time

- On the overhead, show a piece of writing from a child who has included details in his or her picture, and maybe who has started writing.
- Show pieces of literature in which the author puts a lot of detail in the pictures.
- Practice adding details into pictures with a partner.
- Have students watch you as you draw and think aloud about making your illustration tell a story.
- Show children how to look at the details in their pictures to help them write the details. For example, you might say to students, "During reading time, when we get stuck on the words, we sometimes look at the picture for help. In writing, if you get stuck with what to write, you can also look at the picture and write down all that is happening in it."
- "Last night I was admiring your work. I found this beautiful writing," you might say, showing a child's draft. "But then I thought, 'Who is the author?' Then I looked at the next piece of writing and I said, 'Wait! Who is the author of this one?' Soon I had a huge problem because I couldn't tell who the author was on almost any piece! Can you talk to your partner and see if we can invent a solution?" Chances are good that a child will suggest that writers add their names to their writing. A closer inspection will show that, in fact, published authors do just that!

If you look over one child's work and then another's, what you see will vary not only because children vary but because your attention shifts. With one child, you notice volume; with another, you notice punctuation. Sometimes you will want to assign yourself to look across children with one particular lens. For example, notice your children's drawings. Is the child's drawing representational? It is not important whether you can discern exactly what it is that the writer intended to represent, but it is very important that the writer began with a message, and then worked to attach that meaning onto the page. Notice whether the child's drawings suggest that he or she is valuing his or her own life. Rainbows and rows of tulips suggest the child may not use drawing as a way to capture meanings on the page.

Fig. IV-2   Daniel

Daniel's writing [*Fig. IV-2*] doesn't appear representational to me. Daniel may need me to sit alongside him and show him how to remember and record something. After asking what he did yesterday and learning he watched TV, I might say, "What I do is I pretend in my mind that the TV is right here. Show me with your hands how your TV looks." If Daniel doesn't make a shape, I might ask, "Does it look like this?" and use my hands to form a TV. Then I might say, "So I'm picturing that in my mind. Now I'll put it on the paper." Soon I'll ask, "Is there a button to turn it on? Up here?"

Fig. IV-3   Sophie

I suspect that Sophie [*Fig. IV-3*] is drawing what she likes to draw rather than drawing to match a meaning in her mind. You might argue, and rightly so, that there is no big harm with endless stories about butterflies and hearts. But one of the most basic lessons we want to teach writers is that their experiences and ideas are worth putting onto the page.

Fig. IV-4   Joy

Figure IV-4 suggests that Joy uses illustrations to convey stories. She values detail, notices and develops characters, and tries to convey a sequence of action. Joy will need paper that has room for sentences beneath the drawing.

DRAWING EVEN HARD-TO-MAKE IDEAS

GETTING READY

- Chart paper, marker
- Prepared, focused, tiny story in your mind
- See CD-ROM for resources

IN THE PREVIOUS SESSION, YOU SHONE A SPOTLIGHT *on illustrations, showing children detailed and representational drawings by both published authors and classmates. Today's minilesson is an outgrowth of that previous session. Your point then was that writers try to make their drawings carry their content. Today you want to be sure children don't shy away from certain topics because they can't draw those topics.*

This work with children's drawings is really a way to address other issues. Through the medium of illustrations, you are teaching children that writers hold tight to topics they care about and boldly try to write about them, letting nothing stand in their way. You are teaching children that approximation and risk taking are important to the composing process.

Today, you'll encourage children not to worry whether they know how to draw a subject. You'll encourage children to say to themselves, "I'll do the best I can and keep going."

THE MINILESSON

Connection

Tell your children that you sometimes see them hesitate to draw particular topics because they aren't sure how to draw the subject. Tell them you'll show them what you do in that case.

"Writers, I have been so excited about the kinds of things that you have been talking and writing about. But sometimes I see you excited about a great idea, and then you go back to your seats and you're not sure how to draw the picture. And some of you," I frowned sadly, "some of you, *actually decide not to write* about your great idea because you aren't sure how to draw it! That is *so sad* because the world misses out on your wonderful idea. Today I want to show you what I do when I have that 'Oh-oh' feeling."

You catch children's attention by dramatizing extreme versions of the problem.

Teaching

Reenact a writing episode in which you encounter difficulty, consider options for an easier topic, and then decide to persist with the challenging subject.

"I'm going to do a piece of writing and partway through it, you'll see me get that 'Oh-no, I don't know how to draw it!' feeling. I want you to be researchers and watch what I do when I get that feeling."

"I want to tell the story of us opening our window yesterday. Remember how I tried and tried and it was stuck? But we got it open, didn't we? Watch what I do. Notice what happens when I get to tricky parts of my picture."

"Okay, for my story about the stuck window, I'm remembering what happened first. First I tried to open the window and it was stuck. I pushed and pushed."

"Let me start drawing my story. I can make a window, that's easy." I drew a window on the chart paper and then paused, my hand frozen over the picture as if paralyzed. "Oh no! Oh no. I don't know how to show me pushing and

It helps to explicitly tell children what you want them to notice, as I do in this minilesson. I generally avoid launching into a long illustrative example without letting children know why I'm telling this story and what they are to be doing as listeners.

Notice that whenever Leah and I share examples of our writing, our hopes are focused ones. I hope that children learn from the fact that my story is not about the day I went to Disneyland but is instead about the day the window was stuck.

pushing the window. Forget it, I'll just draw a sunny day and flowers. I know how to draw flowers."

Then, pausing dramatically, I shook my head, "No, no, wait a second. No, wait a minute. I'm just going to draw *the best I can*!" I picked up my marker and began to draw a figure shoving the window up. "You can't really tell that much from the picture, but oh well. I'll just *do the best I can and keep going*."

Act out the entire process again, quickly, so the kids see another example of what you mean.

"On this page I want to show what happens next with that window. Remember how a whole bunch of you came up and helped and we *all* shoved till it opened? I'll draw that." I drew the window, and muttered to myself as I did, "That's easy." Then I once again froze in a dramatic fashion. "Oh no. I can't *possibly* draw a whole bunch of kids shoving on the window. Oh no—gosh—I can't draw that. Maybe I'll draw some flowers. I can draw flowers."

Active Engagement

Solicit advice from the class. Have them first tell a friend and then tell you what to do next. Follow their advice.

"Kids, would you tell the person beside you what I could do now. Should I give up and draw flowers?" The room erupts into a hubbub of talk as every child tells another child, 'She should do the best she can.'"

"So Lindsay, what do you think?"

"You should do the best you can!"

"Really? That's what writers do?" I asked as if impressed by this sage advice. "Writers do the best they can and keep going? Wow!" I drew quickly.

Ask children to name what they saw you doing when you got to the tricky part of the drawing.

Now I turned from the chart paper to the class. "What did you notice I did when I got to the tricky part of my picture?"

My story celebrates and gives significance to a tiny event that the class shared together, thus teaching kids that our lives are full of potential stories.

I hope "I'll do the best I can" becomes a mantra for the class and so I make a point of repeating it often in this minilesson and in others.

Of course I'm exaggerating, of course I'm being overly repetitive—but the kids fall for it. By this time in the minilesson the children will feel so smart because they'll know just what is expected of them and they'll be all the more active and engaged.

The kids will be bursting to give you advice. Let them do it—but get them involved by having them all talk to each other, not having just a few talk to you. Notice that I use this active engagement phrase as another chance to reiterate the mantra, "I'll do the best I can and keep going.

Sophie answered, "You tried and tried to draw good and you did not give up!"

Link

Remind the students that you expect they will draw their own pictures the best they can.

"So writers, I'm hoping that today, if you get to a tricky part of your picture, that you will do what I did and just draw it the best you can and not give up!"

MID-WORKSHOP TEACHING POINT

When you see someone try to take the advice of the minilesson, celebrate it by pointing it out to the whole class.

"Oh my gosh, writers, may I stop all of you? Sam is drawing a picture of how his cat's whiskers tickled his belly in the bathtub. He says whiskers are hard for him to draw. I just know he is going to do it the best he can. Oh my gosh, Sam is doing it. He is drawing the whiskers the best he can!"

Don't let too many children talk or the minilesson will become a maxilesson.

Remember to use a signal to get all your writers to stop whatever they are doing and to look at you, silently. Then deliver your message. Don't talk over their voices.

So far, you have learned to make a few absolutely critical moves in your conferences. If you do these while moving efficiently among your children so that you have conferences with six of them within a half hour, you should congratulate yourself. Remember:

▸ Get the child teaching you about his or her content. Draw out more content and then say, "You definitely need to add that!" and help the child to do so in pictures or words—see the conferences cited at right.

▸ Use one-to-one conferences as opportunities to bring your children into the beliefs, values, and traditions of a writing workshop. Say, "Writers do (such and such) . . ." or "During a writing workshop, we. . . ." Do this to foster perseverance, hard work, generosity towards others, and resourcefulness. Remember much of this will be at risk as you push for more print. Try to have a rigorous workshop now when many of them are doing work that comes easily to them.

▸ Pay attention to the flow of the room and to what children can do without you, and learn to record what you see on your unit checklist.

▸ Nudge each child to do what he or she can do with print because it's only after you nudge a child on a bit that you can discern what the child can do. Place each child on your Assessment Checklist at the end of this book and begin to confer with a few in ways that help the child get more print onto the page and give you practice at this sort of teaching.

This conference in *The Conferring Handbook* may be especially helpful today:

▸ *"What's the Story in This Picture?"*

Also, if you have *Conferring with Primary Writers*, you may want to refer to the following conference:

▸ "What's the Story in This Picture?" (all versions)

After-the-Workshop Share

Find a writer who tried the work of the minilesson and have the child tell the rest of the class how it went.

"Remember, today in the minilesson we talked about how writers sometimes get to tricky parts of their pictures and they just do the best they can? Well, today Matthew did that [*Fig. V-1*]. Matthew, would you share what happened today?"

Matthew stood beside me at the front of the meeting area.

"Well, today I was writing about how I went down the slide and I got scared and happy at the same time, because I was going so fast. I didn't know how to draw me going fast, so I just did the best I could and put little lines behind me. I thought that might look like I was going fast."

Remind children they can try the work of this session tomorrow and ever after.

"Tomorrow you can try to do this if you haven't had a chance yet. I know you are eager to draw a hard picture in your mind the best you can."

Often, shares reinforce the minilesson. We can talk until we are blue in the face about how writers draw their pictures the best they can, but sometimes a student who has done that and can articulate what he or she did is the greatest teaching tool of all.

I'd talked to Matthew prior to the share and set him up to say this. Sometimes, it's smart to prep students before they share, so that what they say can become a vital teaching moment for the entire class.

Fig. V-1 Matthew

You may want to teach a second minilesson on this topic. All year, you'll be trying to balance the amount of attention you and the children give to print work and the amount you give to meaning and intention. Your children may need to spend more time on drawing complicated ideas the best they can. If they do, you could try some of the following minilessons.

▸ You could tell the story of a child in the classroom (especially a child who may not otherwise get accolades throughout the day) who persevered and drew a tricky part of her picture. "We've been discussing how, even if we don't know exactly how to draw it, we need to do the best we can when we get to the tricky parts of our pictures. Clarissa did just that yesterday. She wanted to make a story about falling down while rollerblading, but she didn't know how to show herself falling. This is what she did." After showing Clarissa's work, you might involve your children by saying, "Think for a minute about a time when you, like Clarissa, did the best you could. Tell your partner about that time."

▸ You could do a bit of public writing. This time tell children you realized that in a previous piece you left something out because you didn't know how to draw it. Now you could return to that piece and draw in the detail that you'd originally left out because it was hard to draw. You may want, in this instance, to have children bring their folders to the minilesson. "I've noticed that in some of your drawings, you have left out parts of the story." Then you could ask children to get out a finished piece of writing and see if there were details they could add, details that might be hard to draw. "Look at your writing right now." Give them time to look at their texts. "Who found a part they could add on to? Raise your hands. Great. When you are writing today, be brave. Try to draw all the parts of your story the best way that you can. When we come back together, let's share how we tried the tricky parts."

Your workshop will have been underway for about a week now, so this is a good time to pause and reflect on what your children have learned. Reread your goals for the unit and consider your children's progress towards obtaining those goals. Use your conferring checklist to record progress. It will be important to notice whether your children have developed strategies for generating topics they care about. You want them to approach writing brimming with content and eager to use any means possible to convey that content.

If you see a child who approaches writing with fear or who is more preoccupied with writing conventionally correct texts than with conveying content, you'll want to help this child become more committed to his or her content. Listen well, be a receptive reader, and keep your eye on the child's emerging content so the child does the same. Meanwhile, of course, you'll also notice the child's willingness to use print to encode meaning.

The next session is the first in a series designed to nudge every child to use letters to write words. Before you do this teaching, *don't* ask yourself if they are ready. Don't worry whether they know the alphabet or have a handful of sight words. You are going to tell them that writers use pictures and words, knowing full well that some of them will have to approximate or pretend to write. But while pretending to record matching letters, a child can do very real work isolating a word that he or she wants to write, hearing component sounds in that word, and recording one letter for each sound. Meanwhile, the fact that your children are writing (even if their writing consists of diamonds and balloons) will motivate them to learn letters and sounds all the faster.

Using Both Pictures and Words, Like Famous Authors

GETTING READY

- Two familiar books, one that has a picture on each page and a sentence or two accompanying it (perhaps *Corduroy* by Don Freeman) and one that has labeled drawings (like many of Donald Crews' or Richard Scarry's books)
- Writing paper to give each child as he or she *comes* to the minilesson—the paper needs a place for drawing and a place for writing (for kindergartners, probably just one line for writing, for first graders, about four lines)
- Tray of new paper available at each workspace
- See CD-ROM for resources

SOME OF YOUR CHILDREN PROBABLY TELL AND DRAW *their stories but do not write them. Your first goal was to help children put their important stories onto the page, however they conveyed their meaning. You deliberately helped your children become fearless communicators of meaning, so your first lessons were constructed to support children in telling their stories the best they could. Often, this was without print.*

By now, nearly every child should find it easy to choose a topic, envision it, and record it on the page—by some means—working with some independence and tenacity. If this is not yet true for your class, spend a few more days teaching variations of the minilessons in Sessions I to V, either following our suggestions or building your own. However, don't postpone this session more than a week or you'll lose momentum. If your main concern is with whether children are writing or writing enough, continue onward with this session.

Today's minilesson encourages children to write as best they can. If, for one child, this entails listing letters, lollipops, and numbers then that's what you are asking them to do. You can't ask for more than their best!

Children need frequent instruction in sound-letter correspondence to write the letters they need. During other times of the day, you'll teach children to study, admire, and talk about the letters in their names; you'll sing the alphabet song, notice environmental print, and collect items that begin with certain sounds; you'll teach children a few precious sight words such as me and mom. Meanwhile, in the writing workshop, you'll teach children that letters can spell the messages they're dying to get across. As you teach children letters, teach children they need letters.

In this session, you'll remind children that writers write with pictures and words and you'll nudge them to do the same.

THE MINILESSON

Connection

Celebrate that your writers have put their lives onto the page in detailed drawings.

"Writers, I have loved taking your writing home and learning so much about you from your writing. I learned that John plays football and that Anne has a scooter. During writing time, each of you thought of things that you do and that you care about, held those in your mind, then put them on the page. And I can look at your pictures and your stories and learn real details about your life, which is so great!"

Tell children that writers write.

"Now today, I want us all to learn that writers use pictures and words when they write."

Teaching

Show two texts, pointing out that in each the author includes writing.

"Do you all remember this book?" Leah held up *Corduroy* by Don Freeman, a book these children knew well. "You can see that the author, Don Freeman, uses pictures and words to tell this story. Where are the pictures?" They pointed. "Where are the words? Sasha, will you come up and show us where the words are?" She did. "You are right. This author uses pictures and words to tell his story."

"I am telling you this because you can do the same exact thing as this author has done. You can write pictures on the top of your pages and words on the bottom of your pages."

Notice that almost every minilesson begins with the teacher saying "Yesterday we learned . . ." or "I notice that you are . . ." or in some other way, with the teacher naming what children can already do. Usually it helps to cite a very specific example.

Notice the refrain "I'm telling you this because you can do the exact same thing. . . ." You'll find yourself saying this often in your minilessons and conferences!

"Let me show you how another author uses pictures and words. This is one of Donald Crews' books, and I am going to hold it up and ask you to look closely at it. In this book, Donald Crews does it a little differently. He doesn't put his pictures on the top and then his story underneath, does he? He draws his picture and then goes back and he labels some of the important things in the picture. And if you want, you could do what Donald Crews does. You can draw and then write your words as labels. You can do either of these, but you need to have pictures and words in your writing."

Active Engagement

Ask children to point to the place on their pages where they will draw and to the place where they will write.

"You have a new piece of writing paper in front of you. Everyone point to where you will draw your picture. Everyone point to where you are going to put your words." They do.

Link

Remind children to use pictures and words.

"So writers, today I am hoping that each of you will use pictures and words to tell your story."

Leah purposely chooses these two different ways of writing so that all writers in the room have exemplars within their reach. If you are teaching first graders who are experienced writers, you may not need to include labeling as an option. Some children may feel confident about writing more like Don Freeman and others may be more comfortable labeling like Donald Crews does. The second author and second exemplar makes this minilesson multileveled, establishing a range of ways in which children can incorporate print into their texts. The goal is to help all writers feel included in the world of writing.

You will have already handed out paper to the children. If you forgot to do so, hold up a page and ask children to point to the place of that page where you'll draw and then to the place where you'll write.

Leah does not dwell on how the children will get the words down on the page. The purpose of today's lesson is instead to invite children into the world of writing words. Subsequent teaching will address the myriad ways of helping the students in your room become proficient at writing words.

TIME TO CONFER

In this conference, it will be important to pay attention to whether all your children are attempting to write as best they can. Encourage them to do so, following Pathways for guidelines. Remember that every child can write each of the letters as lollipops and diamonds, and remember that whatever the child does when you nudge that child to write is a window onto what that child knows and can do.

You won't have time to work one-to-one with every child, but you'll want every child to know that pressure is on to write. You can take some time to just move among writers, crouching at a table, and saying, "I want to admire the way you are all writing both pictures and words. Would you each point to your picture? Would you point to your words? Congratulations for having both."

 These conferences in *The Conferring Handbook* may be especially helpful today:

▶ *"What's the Story in This Picture?"*
▶ *"Where Is Your Writing?"*
▶ *"Let Me Show You How to Write More"*

Also, if you have *Conferring with Primary Writers,* you may want to refer to the conferences in part one.

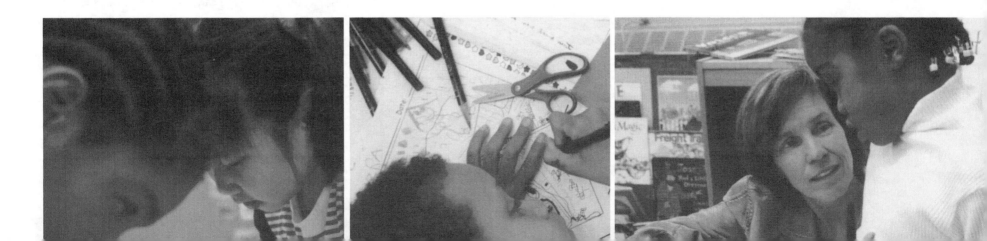

AFTER-THE-WORKSHOP SHARE

Fig. VI-1   Deleana

My mom said, "Cut it out." My mom said, "Cut it out!"
My mom said, "Cut it out!" I love my mom. I love my mom.

When children have gathered together again, ask one student to read his or her writing to the rest of the class.

Leah gathered the children on the carpet, and each child sat in his or her rug spot. "Today I saw so many of you doing what writers do." Leah kept Deleana and Liam near her and signaled to Deleana to stand beside her, facing the class. Deleana held her work for all to see.

"Would you read it to us?" Leah asked, fully aware that Deleana hadn't written with sound-letter correspondence.

Deleana pointed to her letters (a good step), and, as she pointed to each line, she "read" a line. [*Fig. VI-1*]

Ask the students to talk to each other about what they noticed about that student's work.

"Writers, would you tell your partner the smart work you saw Deleana doing?"

After a bit, Leah bypassed raised hands, "I heard some of you notice that she has a place for her pictures and a place for her words, and you are right. That is smart work. And Deleana reread it with her finger, paying attention to her writing. Thank you, Deleana."

Select a few more students to read their writing. Make sure all children in the class realize that they have the ability to write as best they can.

"I'm so happy to see the writing you all have put on your pages. So many of you tried to not only draw, but to write like Don Freeman or Donald Crews! Next time we have a chance to write, we can all put our writing on our page with our pictures!"

It's important to set up the expectation that every child will have something on his or her paper that can be "read" to the rest of the class. In a conference held before the share, Leah had made sure Deleana could "read" her writing to the class.

It's important to select students who have managed to do something that is not drawing that can be read. It is also important to choose a range of ability so that the less-proficient writers realize that writing is writing is writing, and that the best they can do is writing too if they intend their marks as words that carry meaning.

Your children will certainly need more help recording words, and you will certainly devote more minilessons to this. You could move onto the next session or develop another minilesson.

▶ You might tell the class that you will work together to do some shared writing. "Today, we are going to write a whole-class piece of writing, and we'll include both pictures and words. Let's write about the cat we saw run across the playground yesterday. So I am going to get started with the picture. I need to draw the cat. And the playground. What else?" After eliciting a response or two, you might say, "Okay, now, let's start our writing— let's do what Donald Crews does and put a label or two. What should we label?" You would elicit several responses and write a label or two. "Okay, now let's write a sentence at the bottom. Hmmm. Let's write, 'We saw a cat run across the playground.'" You would need to this quickly, without laboring over the words too much.

▶ You could say, "Lots of you have been working hard to add words to your pictures. I have noticed that many of you have tried to label, like Donald Crews. That is wonderful." You could show a couple of examples from kid's work on previous days. "I did some labeling, just like Donald also." You could show prepared writing, with labels only. "Here I am brushing my hair. Now I want to stretch myself as a writer and add some words, a sentence, just like Don Freeman did. I think I'll write, 'I am fixing my hair.'" After you do this, you could ask, "I'm wondering how many of you feel that you could really stretch yourselves as writers today and try adding some words under the pictures, like Don Freeman did in *Corduroy*? Raise your hands if you think you can. It's great to see so many of you with your hands raised! I can't wait to see your work!"

Your instinct may be to gather your children's texts and to look them over, categorizing children into groups based on what they do with print. Some, like the child we studied in the preceding session, will write with random strings of letters. Don't push Deleana's piece [*Fig. VI-1*] aside as if it shows nothing. You will want to observe how a child who writes random strings reads this sort of writing. Does she have a sense that texts are read left to right, top to bottom? Does she seem to think that more marks on the page means a longer utterance? When she "reads" a message, does it sound like a written text, or does it sound conversational? Is the text stable, so that each time she "rereads" it, the text says roughly the same things?

In this instance, Deleana reveals that she has a sense for many print conventions. She has some sense of literary language (although it is unclear how or whether her text fits together as a cohesive whole). It's important to keep in mind that Deleana's text does not suggest that she has no ability to make sound-symbol correspondences. She hasn't made sound-symbol correspondences *in this instance*, but I'd want to ask her if the big figure in the picture is her mom, and to get her to say *mom* slowly, to think, "What sound do you hear first?" and to record that sound—because I have a hunch she could do so just fine!

Jordan [*Fig. VI-2*], of course, is in a very different place than Deleana when it comes to print.

His spellings are quite conventional. It's impressive that he spells *apple*, *lunch*, and *outside* correctly. It is intriguing that he finds the concrete word *apple* easier to spell than more nebulous words such as *then* or *had*. Although Jordan's spellings are quite well developed, he often writes with uppercase letters. I'd tell him not to do this. More significantly, he seems to think that writing involves captioning pictures. ("This is the lunch. I am having bread.")

Fig. VI-1   Deleana

My mom said, "Cut it out." My mom said, "Cut it out!" My mom said, "Cut it out!" I love my mom. I love my mom.

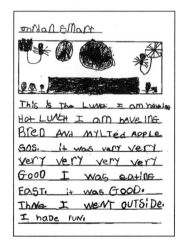

Fig. VI-2   Jordan

This is the lunch. I am having hot lunch. I am having bread and my little apple sauce. It was very very very very very very good. I was eating fast. It was good. Then I went outside. I had fun.

STRETCHING AND WRITING WORDS

GETTING READY

- Chart paper, marker
- Story idea
- Pile of familiar books that have pictures and words
- Materials for children to write during the minilesson and share—white boards or individual paper and writing utensils
- See CD-ROM for resources

USUALLY WHEN YOU TEACH, FIRST YOU INTRODUCE STUDENTS *to the big picture of what they'll be doing, and then you help them with the necessary fine points of that work. In the last session, you urged them all to include pictures and words. Now you'll want to help them with the fine points of doing that work.*

The goal in this particular minilesson is to teach the strategies writers use when they want to go from having a content in mind to writing a word on the page. In this minilesson, you will demonstrate one way to do this: Writers decide what they'll write, isolate the first word, say it and sound it out, write the first sound, reread it, hear more sounds, and so on until the word is represented on the page to the writer's satisfaction.

This is a basic, introductory lesson to the concept of translating sounds into print. For experienced writers, you might alter this so that you demonstrate that different strategies are used with different words. Some words are ones we use a lot and we just know them (or use the word wall as a reference), and sometimes we use words we know to help with words we don't know.

In this session, then, you'll help writers separate out the many sounds they hear in words and write down the letters that correspond to those sounds.

Connection

Tell children they are writing like the authors they admire. Tell them you'll teach them how to write words.

"Writers, I took your writing home last night and it felt like I'd taken a big pile of books home from our library," I said. I held up familiar books by Charlotte Zolotow, Eric Carle, and Bill Martin. "Just like these authors write about all sorts of things—a caterpillar, a dance, a girl looking in the mirror—you kids write about all sorts of things. And just like these authors use pictures *and* words, most of you do that too. We'll keep working on that. Now watch how I decide what letters to put on the page when I'm writing my words."

Teaching

Write publicly, demonstrating what you want children to try.

"I first decided to write about a wooden boat I made, so on this page I drew the boat floating. And on this page, I show that I added a lot of things onto the boat and it tipped over. Now, I'm going to write in front of you. Watch how I write my words."

Shifting into role of being a child, I said, "Umm. I think I'll write, 'I made a boat.' Okay. *I.*" I muttered, "That's easy." I wrote *I.* "Let me reread," and I did, with my finger under my print. I then articulated the still-unwritten word *made.* Breaking it down, I said, "/m/" and wrote *m.* I again reread with my finger under the letters *I m* and soon I'd progressed to saying /ade/, /ade/." I wrote *ad* and again reread.

"Did you notice that I first said what I wanted to write, then I broke it down to just the first word—then I wrote and reread that? Then I said the next word—I broke down the sounds. And I wrote the sound and again I reread."

In this minilesson, as in most, I begin by naming what children are already doing and by citing a particular example or two. Then my connection ends with me saying, "Today I'll show you . . ." and explicitly telling children what I hope they will learn. This is the way every minilesson goes.

Notice that this isn't an especially ambitious lesson. Especially at this early stage in the year, the most important thing is to begin nudging all children to write words and to do this while maintaining lots of support for the most vulnerable writers. I do not want to lose students,

Active Engagement

Ask children to join you in writing the sounds you hear in the words you write.

"Will you help me to keep going? First I'll reread what I wrote. Let's do that together." I waited for the class to be with me, and together, with my finger under the print, we read, "'I made. . . . ' Now let's say and write what's next—*a*. On your hands," I pointed to the palm of my hand, "pretend to write that word and I'll do it up here." I wrote *a*. "Now what do we do? We reread, don't we? Let's do it together. 'I made a. . . . '"

"Boat!" the children said. I pointed to the place on the paper where I'd soon write *boat* and moved my hands as I said the word slowly and fluidly (not in a stacatto /b/ /o/ /t/). "Say it with me," I said. "We are stretching the word like a rubber band." After saying *boooaaat* together a few times, I said, "What sound do you hear first?" /b/? Okay. We hear a /b/ sound and that is spelled with a *b*. Soon the class had written *bot*, and reread the sentence.

Link

Tell children to try on their own what you have done together.

"Today, try to write words on your page, just like real authors do. Say them, stretch them out, write what you hear, reread and say more."

MID-WORKSHOP TEACHING POINT

Point out the initiative of a student who has done some independent revision.

"Jose did something so smart. He wrote a story about how he took the subway to the baseball game," I showed one page, "and then he realized he needed another page to show what happened when he got there! So he got another page from the writing center and he stapled it. May I show you how he did it?"

---

but I do want to give a sense of how to approach spelling. In this minilesson, I do not ask for student input. This will prolong the lesson too much and divide the class into "those who know" and "those who don't know." I want to avoid these situations as much as possible and to make every effort to be sure every learner feels welcome as part of the "club."

The correct spelling is, of course, boat, and if children are quite mature as spellers, you may decide to tell them that actually, the word is spelled a little differently than it sounds. This is a judgement call. If it is a new thing for most of your children to listen for the record sounds at all, you won't want to emphasize the silent a.

Sometimes, you can interrupt the workshop like this to tell students about a wonderful new development in the flow of the class's work—something initiated by a student. And you may follow through with a demonstration of how to staple. Of course, make sure you call attention to many different students, eventually all of them, over time.

TIME TO CONFER

In this conference, you may want to do three things. First, take a little step back and notice the flow of your room now. You've raised the stakes and probably made some writers feel needy. Don't push your writers so hard that they can no longer carry on with independence and engagement, because if your children all become dependent, you won't be free to do the teaching you need to do.

It is important to continue to help many children identify what they want to say, to select their first word, to say that word slowly, and to record sounds. A large percentage of children will need one-to-one help with this. You'll be talking-up the importance of this in your minilessons, but the minilessons will fly right past your children unless you also provide this one-to-one support. See conferences cited at right.

If you feel it's urgent to get to your kids to support their work with print, try gathering four kids together into print-based strategy lessons. Use *A Strategy Lesson* in the *Conferring with Primary Writers* book as a resource. If a child has attempted to write "I love my mom" and has written just a few letters, feel free to record the intended message in cursive (as a note to yourself) along the edge of the paper. If the child acts interested, dismiss what you've done saying, "It's just a note to myself."

Remember that when you push for letters and sounds, some children may go overboard and begin copying print from the classroom, writing only stories they can spell, or using similar strategies. Continue to focus on choosing a topic that writers know and care about, drawing the content first, saying the oral text aloud, and only then writing. See "What's the Story in This Picture?" in *The Conferring Handbook* and all three versions of this conference in the *Conferring with Primary Writers* book.

These conferences in *The Conferring Handbook* may be especially helpful today:

- ▶ *"Where Is Your Writing?"*
- ▶ *"Let Me Show You How to Write More"*
- ▶ *"What's the Story in This Picture?"*

Also, if you have *Conferring with Primary Writers*, you may want to refer to the following conferences:

- ▶ "Let Me Help You Put Some Words Down"
- ▶ "What's the Story in This Picture?" (all versions)

After-the-Workshop Share

Choose a child to tell the story of his or her process of stretching out a long or hard word to write it down.

"I was noticing how Raphael was writing *electric train* because he was telling the story of getting his train. At first he thought, 'I don't know how to write *electric*. That's a big word.' So Raphael, will you tell us what you did to write that big word?"

Raphael said, "Well, I said it slowly with my mouth, *electric*, and I wrote an e because I heard an /e/ at the beginning. Then I heard a c in the middle so I wrote c and then I heard another c at the end so I wrote another c."

Ask children to reread their work to reflect on their own writing process to see if it matched, or could match, the one explained.

"Writers, would you read what you wrote today to yourselves?" I paused. "Did anyone else do what Raphael did and try a word you didn't know?"

If the children need it, choose another student to explain another example of the same process.

"What did you write [*Fig. VII-1*], Hannah?"
"I wrote *dolphin* cause I really watched one, a real one."

Ask everyone to try, with a partner, this process of stretching out a word to write it. Suggest the word for everyone to try.

"Class, let's all try to do what Hannah did. I'm going to pass out white boards and would you help each other and see if some of you can write *dolphin* on your white boards?"

You will have talked with the student you have chosen in a conference during independent writing time. That way, the child will have used the words to describe his or her process already. This helps keep share time short and to the point.

Fig. VII-1   Hannah

Dolphins Jump High

Choose a word that excites children and that everyone can write together—help them feel they can write any word in the world they want to write. Allow approximations. The point isn't to learn to spell a particular word correctly.

It is clear that children will need more time working with the strategies you've just demonstrated in this minilesson. You could plan to do other minilessons that are variations of it, but the most important forum for teaching this is one-to-one conferences and small-group strategy lessons. In follow-up minilessons, you might do any of these things.

▸ If you did a demonstration in which you wrote sentences on each page in a book, you may want to show children that sometimes instead you and other writers write labels. "Can you help me label my drawing? The picture shows me on the swings at the park. What could I write?" Soon you could have children working on white boards to help you write *grass* or *me*.

▸ Tell the story of a child who bravely "had a go" with a new word. You can describe the process the child went through. "Yesterday I saw Greg do a really great job with a tricky word. He was trying to write *birthday*. He said the word really slowly, like this." You demonstrate. "He wrote the first sound he heard. Then he said it again. He wrote the next sound. Then, he did this really smart thing. He went back and reread with his finger to make sure he got all the sounds. Great job. Who thinks they can do this same kind of brave work like Greg? Raise your hands. Great."

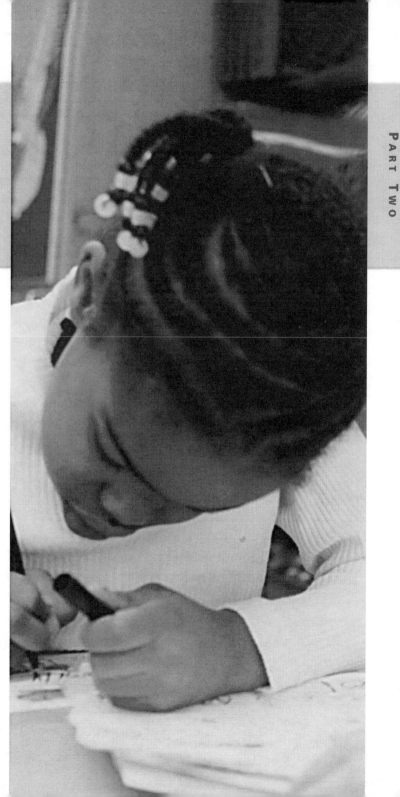

STRETCHING AND WRITING WORDS: INITIAL SOUNDS

GETTING READY

▶ Chart paper, marker
◉ See CD-ROM for resources

THE PREVIOUS SESSION ENCOURAGED CHILDREN *to stretch out words and record the sounds they hear. Some of your students will have started to listen to sounds in words and to write these sounds down as letters during writing workshop. Others have some knowledge of sounds and letters that they are not yet drawing on during writing workshop.*

Still others may not yet understand the concept of listening for sounds.

One five-year-old wanted to write the word Santa. Her teacher said, "Say the word slowly. Ssaannta. Ssaannta. What sounds do you hear?" The child repeated the word again, as if listening hard. "Ssaannta," she said. "I hear 'ho ho ho!'"

This minilesson aims to help students develop another strategy for getting words down on paper—listening hard to the beginning sounds of words to write those and give the reader a good start on the word.

For now, you will show students how to listen hard to how words start so that they can get those first letters down on the page for their readers.

THE MINILESSON

Connection

Tell children you'll show them a way to get started writing, building on what they've already learned.

"I know that we've been talking about writing our words the best we can. And we've been talking about stretching out words so that we can hear the sounds in them. Today I want to show you how to get the main sounds you hear in your words down on the paper."

Teaching

Return to a piece of writing you've used previously in a minilesson and say aloud a new bit you want to add.

"Today I want to work on my writing about me running over the Brooklyn Bridge with my friend Jane. I remembered that Jane told me to be careful because she saw a car coming. So I think I will write 'Please be careful' in a speech bubble above Jane."

Tell children to watch how you get the words onto the page.

"Watch me say the words and write down the sounds I hear. Later I'm going to ask you to help me."

"Hmmm. *Please.* Let me say the word and write down what I hear in the beginning, /pl/. I hear a *p*."

"*Please.* Let me say it again and listen to what else I hear. *Please.* What can I hear at the beginning of the word? P-l, P, L. I hear an *l*. Let me write that down." Leah wrote an l beside her p. She reread, pointing at her letters and saying, "*Please.*" I hear an /s/ too!" She wrote this.

"*Be.* What do I hear at the beginning? That's easy, I hear a *b*!"

By the end of the connection, children should know exactly what the teacher will teach today.

Notice that Leah chooses the words she will write and doesn't enlist the help of her students in this. This minilesson is designed to teach students to listen to sounds in words. Leah doesn't want to take time to have a long conversation about the content of her piece. Such a conversation takes the students away from the focus of this lesson.

Leah is not hoping to teach the correct spelling of please, *but instead she wants to teach children to hear and try to record at least the beginning and ending sounds in a word. If many of her students wrote with more sounds, she'd demonstrate a higher level of skill.*

Retell the process you used to record words. Tell children to use the same process.

"Children, did you notice I said the word and wrote down what I heard at the start of it? Then I said the word again and wrote down what I heard next. I'm telling you that because you can do the same thing."

Active Engagement

Assign them a word and ask them to try the process with you.

"Let's try it together with the word *careful*. Say the word *careful*. What do you hear at the beginning? Justin, what is the sound that you hear at the beginning?" Justin said *l*. "Justin, there is an *l* at the end of *careful*. What do you hear at the beginning of the word?" Justin said the sound /kkkk/ and then the letter *k*. "Yes, I do hear a /k/ sound at the beginning of careful. And yes, *k* does make the /k/ sound! Let's write a *k* the way Justin suggested. There are more sounds in *careful*. Everyone say the word and listen for more sounds." They did.

"I hear an /r/," Jose said. "I hear that too! /r/. Okay, let me write that down." Leah did.

Tell children to continue writing on their own, using this same process.

"What you are doing is smart. Keep on rereading and saying, 'Are there more sounds I could record?' because this is a good start to *careful*, but it sounds like it has more letters, don't you think? Work with your friend and try to think about what comes next."

Link

Remind children of today's lesson so that they can carry it into their independent work. Tell them to get started by listening for the beginning sounds of words, then to listen to more.

"So today, when you are writing your words, could you make sure that you say the word once and write down what you hear in the beginning, and then say the word again and write down the other sounds you hear?"

Notice that Leah is precise with her language and stays with her original teaching point of helping students listen for and record sounds in words, especially the initial sounds.

Leah does some important things here. She chooses a specific strategy: Say the word and write down what you hear at the beginning and then say the word again and write what you hear later in the word.

Since the goal of the lesson is not to teach children the correct spelling of careful *but instead to teach them how to listen closely to the beginning and middle of words to get those sounds down, many teachers would respond to Justin with affirmation and encouragement. After all, he has done a great deal correctly, even if the initial suggestion that* careful *begins with a* k *isn't correct.*

TIME TO CONFER

So far, I've tried to encourage you to use conferences to remind writers that writing is always about having a message, and then putting that message onto the page. I've tried to nudge you to help children develop and record their messages.

But your focus during conferences must be a double one, because while you cultivate your children's growth as writers, you must also cultivate *your* growth as a teacher of writing. You may want to pay attention to the architecture of conferences. Do this by rereading the chapter about conferring in *The Nuts and Bolts of Teaching Writing* and attending to the predictable components of conferences. You may want to use the guide sheet (see CD-ROM) for support. Notice that every conference begins with research and that, in the midst of research, you will want to name what the child has done that is really, really smart. It's a trick to do this well. You may want to read through a whole lot of conferences, zeroing in on only this particular conference move. Then, as you confer, work on getting good at doing just this one, essential teaching move. The same teaching move occurs at the end of a conference in the link.

These conferences in *The Conferring Handbook* may be especially helpful today:

- ▶ *"What's the Story in This Picture?"*
- ▶ *"Where Is Your Writing?"*
- ▶ *"Let Me Show You How to Write More"*

Also, if you have *Conferring with Primary Writers*, you may want to refer to the conferences in part one.

AFTER-THE-WORKSHOP SHARE

Share with students the writing of one of their classmates, which can get them excited about where their own writing is going. In this case, you might share a piece of writing that is very long.

"Writers, I want to share what happened to some of you today. When some of you listened and wrote down the sounds you heard, you got a lot on your paper. That's what happened to Clarissa today [*Fig. VIII-1*]. She wrote her words and she kept writing and writing. Listen!"

Imply with excitement that everyone could soon be doing what this child has done.

"Someday, maybe you all can try writing more and more and more!"

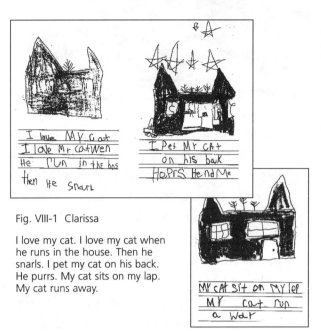

Fig. VIII-1 Clarissa

I love my cat. I love my cat when he runs in the house. Then he snarls. I pet my cat on his back. He purrs. My cat sits on my lap. My cat runs away.

Getting a lot on the paper is addressed in future minilessons. Occasionally, you might use the share, as Leah does here, to briefly introduce what will be taught in detail in future minilessons. This can build excitement in the children and can also serve as a reinforcing preview of lessons to come.

▶ If most of your children are now writing a sentence under their drawing, you can tell them they have graduated. They no longer need plain, blank paper because now they always write sentences to go with their drawings. You can make this into a graduation party because they are all moving on to more grownup paper. This may give a helpful push to the few who need it.

▶ You may want to spend another day doing some public writing in which your emphasis on letters and sounds is contextualized inside an emphasis on having a story to tell. You don't want to overstress stretching out words, hearing all the sounds, or using alphabet charts without also making sure that your students understand the most important things about writing. Your first goal is to be sure they all know writers fill themselves with all that they have to say. Then writers put what they can on the page and keep going, trying to say a lot. You want students to be fluent and independent at their less-than-complete approximations of writing before you begin pushing them to hear a great many sounds in a word. For example, you might tell children that you're going to write about something true. Putting a blank page on the easel, you might say, "Hmmm. I think I'll make a story about a cat I saw today on my way to school." As you talk, you would draw a cat. "She was skinny. I could see her ribs." Now, drawing a person alongside the cat, you add, "She followed me." In deliberately writing about a small everyday event, the sort of event that every one of your children has experienced personally, one of the messages is that we all have stories to tell. *Then* you work with sounds.

You'll want to take your children's work home and categorize your children into clusters based on what you want to say to them:

▶ Some will have heard your encouragement to draw with detail and gone overboard. Their drawings may be so time-consuming that these children are not spending much time on writing. The joy of markers on paper may have enticed some children into decorating every dress and coloring every blade of grass. For others, drawings may be a refuge from writing. You probably want to allow children to draw with absorption for now because this keeps them busy and the workshop productive. But meanwhile, be sure you interrupt these children and ask them to write. "What do you want to say? So write that while I'm here." The fact that some children are happily and productively busy drawing will give you the time to work with other individuals to develop their abilities to write words.

▶ Some children will write what seems to you at least to be random strings of letters. Catch these children in the act so you can discern if these letters are, in fact, random. A child could say, "I ride my bike to the store. I got bread," and use sound-symbols somewhat correctly (but incompletely) to record IRDMB2USRIGTBD. Chances are that such a child will have forgotten what he or she wrote and that you will conclude erroneously that the child copied any letters he or she saw, all in a row, with no reliance on phonics.

The trick is to catch a child in the act of writing so you can understand the logic that informs the child.

▶ Some children will write by recording at least one letter for the major sounds they hear. These children are well on their way. They'll benefit from learning new word chunks, from learning high frequency words, and from using a variety of strategies to spell as best they can.

SPELLING THE BEST WE CAN ... AND MOVING ON

GETTING READY

- Chart paper, marker
- Prepared drawing
- White boards and dry erase markers for each child
- Extra writing paper
- See CD-ROM for resources

WRITERS, LIKE READERS, NEED TO KEEP A FIRM HOLD ON MEANING *while still doing a lot of work with the print on a page. Teaching, then, is a balancing act. For a few days, our teaching emphasizes that writers envision their subjects, write from the true happenings in their lives, and include a lot of detail so readers will understand their meaning. Then we "run to the other side of the boat" and tell writers to stretch out their words, to hear and record more sounds, to reread often as they progress through the spelling of a word, and so on.*

You'll need to keep an eye on your class to determine which emphasis is needed now. If children are beginning to let their knowledge of words constrain their content, you'll want to return their attention to the importance of envisioning their subject and drawing in ways that tell the truth. On the other hand, if your children are drawing up a storm, you may need to remind them that after they draw a page, it's important to write the words. Perhaps you need to do a minilesson that essentially revisits the minilesson you did in Session VII, perhaps this time with an emphasis on hearing not only initial but also final sounds.

In this session, you'll teach writers to accept their own approximate spellings in order to tell more about their stories. The mantra is, "Writers do the best they can and keep going."

THE MINILESSON

Connection

Remind children that they've previously learned to draw the best they can and keep going. Tell them this idea applies to spelling as well.

"A few days ago we talked about drawing the best we can and not worrying if we felt like we couldn't do it. When we don't know how to draw our topics we say, 'I'll draw my best,' and we know we'll get better because we are working on it. Samantha didn't know how to show her dog curled up to sleep, but she said, 'I'll try' and did the best she could."

"Today I want to remind you that when we write words, we need to say, 'That might not be perfect yet, but I'll just spell the best I can and keep going so I can say more.' You can get a lot of writing done when you write your words the best you can and keep going."

This is a lesson you might well want to use in every subject area. Children cannot be afraid to take risks and make mistakes or their learning throughout their lives will suffer. Children need to learn that every kind of thinking and learning, in every discipline, involves making less-than-perfect drafts and building from them.

Teaching

Demonstrate hesitating, trying to spell a hard word, and then continuing on to write more.

"Today I thought I'd write the words to go with my picture about the stuck window in our classroom, and I want you to watch what I do when I get to tricky words." I turned the chart paper back to the drawing from Session V. "I think I'll write, 'I pushed and shoved on our window but it wouldn't budge.'" Then I began dictating to myself and writing. I moved quickly, every now and then hemming and hawing about how to spell a word, but then I shrugged, "Oh well. I'll leave it like that for now and keep going." In this fashion, I fairly quickly wrote the sentence and turned to the next picture.

Notice that I do not solicit help from the children at this stage. In part I am trying to demonstrate speed, and so pausing for contributions is counterproductive. There are times to solicit children's input and times when doing so makes lessons harder to understand.

Active Engagement

Point out to the children what you want them to notice in your demonstration. Invite them to help you go through the process again.

"Did you see how I just did the best I could and kept going? I'm going to give you white boards so you can join me in doing this for the next page." I passed a white board and dry erase marker to each child.

"I think I'll say, 'Soon half the class was shoving on the window. Finally it opened.' Let's do this together. I'll say the word, you kids write it the best you can. *Soon*," I paused. "*half*," I paused. "*The*—you know *the*," I paused. "*class*," I paused.

"Writers, let's stop for a second. Hold up your boards so I can admire what you did!" They did. "Look how much you got down! Let's read what we've written. Everyone put your finger under the first word *soon*. Let's read it and keep going." They did.

Link

Remind the children that they can do this again in their independent writing.

"Today, remember, if you want to put something on the paper and you aren't sure how to draw it or how to write it—just," I invited the children to chime in, "'Do the best you can and keep going,' right?"

You'll want to decide whether to distribute white boards at this moment or to do so at the start of the minilesson.

TIME TO CONFER

By now, you have a wonderful, plentiful repertoire of conferences. You know how to conduct what I call content conferences—see "What's the Story in This Picture?" (three versions)—and expectation conferences—see "Why Don't You Write a Sign for the Block Area?" and "Where is Your Writing Work?" in the *Conferring with Primary Writers* book. You are able to coach writers to listen to and record words—see "Where is Your Writing?" and "Let Me Show You How to Write More" in *The Conferring Handbook* and "Help a Child Move from Strings of Random Letters to Labels" in *Conferring with Primary Writers* book. You also know something about leading small-group strategy lessons. Use all of this!

You also have a growing list of topics that you've taught in minilessons, shares, and previous conferences. You need to refer back to prior teaching if you want your children to do so. For example, don't forget:

- Your children are writing like real authors. Some, like Richard Scarry, have pictures with labels. Some have pictures on the top of a page and words underneath.
- Writers choose topics and write what they know about.
- Writers first think of a topic, envision it, and then draw it.
- Writers know that when they are finished, they have more to do.
- Writers go back and add more detail.
- Writers take care of their tools.
- Writers write words.
- Writers say, "I'll do the best I can and keep going."

These conferences in *The Conferring Handbook* may be especially helpful today:
- *"Where Is Your Writing?"*
- *"Let Me Show You How to Write More"*

Also, if you have *Conferring with Primary Writers*, you may want to refer to the following conferences:
- "What's the Story in This Picture?" (all versions)
- "Where is Your Writing Work?"
- "Why Don't You Write a Sign for the Block Area?"
- "Let Me Help You Put Some Words Down"

AFTER-THE-WORKSHOP SHARE

Choose children who took the minilesson to heart, whether they enacted the advice exactly or found new solutions, and ask them to tell the class about their experience.

I waited until all eyes were on me. "Writers, today Zoë and Joseph are going to share. They're sharing because they both came to hard parts when they were writing their words, and they did the best they could and just kept going. You're not going to believe how much they got done!"

"Here's Zoë's piece." [*Fig. IX-1*]

"Zoë couldn't remember the word *sled*. She used the word *thingamajig* as a placeholder and kept on writing her story."

"Now, Joseph is going to read his piece." [*Fig. IX-2*]

I went on an airplane. I had to go to the bathroom and my mom went in the bathroom with me. I was so mad. She thought I was too small to go by myself.

As always, point out to the children what you hope they noticed in the reading or demonstration; show how the example demonstrates the lesson.

"Look how Joseph wrote the best he could and then just kept going so his ideas could get written on the paper!"

You will, of course, have been on the lookout during the workshop time for students who could share in a helpful way with their peers. The share time is an orchestrated teaching moment, not a random report-back session.

I went on my thingamajig. My brother was screaming when we went down the hill, but he didn't fall.

Fig. IX-1   Zoë

When Joseph read his piece, he began at the left and moved his finger across the squiggles. Because Joseph has not yet grasped the idea of letters, he uses squiggles as placeholders. He nevertheless has written and told a long story.

Fig. IX-2   Joseph

- Ask students to go into their folders to choose a piece of writing which contains trick words. Perhaps they bypassed some of those words earlier. Would they be willing to try them now?
- Challenge children to be brave, to tackle hard words. "Today I watched Margo. She was writing about art and wanted to say she made an origami bird but she realized that *origami* was a hard word. Do you know what she did? She said, 'Oh well. I'll try it anyway!' Let's all try that word. On your white boards, would you try to write *origami*."

ASSESSMENT

Most early childhood standards put great emphasis on children developing "approaches to learning." Over half of children enter kindergarten with impressive item knowledge. Sixty-six percent of children know their alphabet letters, can count to ten, and can distinguish upper- and lowercase letters. But far fewer children enter kindergarten with the curiosity and tenacity and energy that make them ready for school learning. These qualities are hard to assess, but they matter more than anything. Now, in September of the year, you really want to watch whether your children approach writing with zeal, energy, and passion. What is their receptivity to learning written language? Do they act enthusiastic when it is time for writing? They should. Do they seem willing to "write" for ever longer durations? They should.

When you reflect on each child's developing abilities to word solve, it's also wise to keep in mind what matters most.

▶ To what extent is this child an active, resourceful, engaged learner? Some children will have entered your classroom with more experience with print and will display more item knowledge. Don't fool yourself into thinking that a child who knows more is necessarily learning more quickly or showing more capacity to learn. This child may simply have begun learning about letters before other children. Watch for and celebrate engagement, a willingness to take risks, a resourcefulness, and delight. Watch, also, to see if a child is able to hold tight to meaning while also working with print.

▶ Over time, you want to see clear evidence that each child is progressing as a word solver. The growth is usually very evident and pronounced. If a child seems to not be moving forward in this dimension, make a point to work with that child individually several times a week.

USING WRITING TOOLS: THE ALPHABET CHART

GETTING READY

- Enlarged alphabet chart with easily identifiable pictures to correspond with the letters—children should already be familiar with this chart
- Chart paper, marker
- Copy of alphabet chart (or name chart or word wall) for each child to have on hand while writing
- See CD-ROM for resources

IN EVERY UNIT OF STUDY, YOU WILL INTRODUCE A TOOL *or two that remains throughout the rest of the year, often as a physical embodiment of the original unit of study. Thus far in this unit, you've introduced the "When I'm Done" chart. In this minilesson, we introduce the alphabet chart and make sure that each child has one nearby as he or she writes.*

You may decide that this is not the time to give children individual copies of the alphabet chart. If your children are kindergartners and you have worked extensively with them on their names, you may decide to give each child an individual copy of the name chart to use instead of the alphabet chart. The word wall could also work here. Children need to be comfortable enough with the alphabet chart that there is a good chance they can use it on the run as they write. If the tool is too overwhelming, its presence can debilitate your children, and the tool's future helpfulness may be lessened.

For today's session, you will show students how to match the sound they hear in the word they want to write with a letter that represents it, using an alphabet chart with pictures for help.

THE MINILESSON

Connection

Remind children of their work with the enlarged alphabet chart, and tell them you'll teach them to use this chart as they write.

"Writers, remember how we have studied this chart and used it to help us find and write letters? Today I want to show you how we can use this chart during writing workshop."

Teaching

Think aloud as you write, demonstrating how the alphabet chart is a useful tool.

"Watch me write, and notice how I use this chart. We'll talk in a few minutes about what you notice." Then Leah began to write on chart paper. She paused, her pen poised for a moment, "I want to write about having a fancy dinner at my sister's house. My brother was acting silly and kept trying to make me laugh. I'm going to sketch the picture." Leah drew quickly, saying nothing to embellish the story.

"Okay, I want to write, 'At the fancy dinner, I never should have sat near Josh.'" Leah dictated each word quietly to herself. She wrote the first few words easily and paused over *have*. Leah read what she'd written. "At the fancy dinner, I never should have. . . *have*. Let me read through the pictures on this chart until I find one that starts like /h/. Hey, *have* starts like *hat*." Leah motioned to the *h* on the alphabet chart, and wrote an *h*. She continued to work quickly until she came to *near*. "*Near*. . . /r/. I always forget that /r/ sound." A few students called out *r*, but Leah pretended she didn't hear them. "Remember, your job is to watch what I do to help myself. Soon I'll ask what you noticed that I did."

"Hmmm. *Near.. . /r/.*" She turned to the alphabet chart. "Okay, it's not like *peach*, /p/, *queen*, /kw/ no. . . *rrrabbit*, /r/. *Nearrrr*, /r/. Hey, the /r/ is just like *rabbit*." She pointed to the picture on the chart.

Leah has already introduced the whole-class alphabet chart. You probably will want to hold off on this minilesson until you have done the same for your children.

Leah does not add verbal embellishment to her story since the focus of the lesson is on writing the words.

Many of the minilessons in this particular unit of study are cut out of the same cloth. Leah says, "Let me teach you what I do when I write." Then she composes in front of her class, articulating her quandaries—the ones she expects students to have. Then she or a child names what she has done and she invites writers to use similar strategies in their writing. As the year progresses, there will be a greater variety to the minilessons, but this will remain a staple.

"Okay, let me look at the rabbit part of this chart to find what that letter looks like. Hmmm," Leah looked at the *r* for a moment and then wrote an r on her page. "*Near*, /r/, ends with an *r*, like /r/*abbit*," she said aloud to further demonstrate her point. Leah continued to write, not stopping many times. In this demonstration, she sometimes spelled by approximating "as best she could," and she sometimes stopped to use the chart.

Active Engagement

Ask the students what they noticed.

"So, how did I use the chart to help me?"

"You wanted to write *have,* you found *hat* and copied it," Patrick said.

"You're right, when I was writing the word *have* I couldn't remember how to write the /h/ and then I saw that *hat* and *have* both start with that sound." Leah pointed to the picture of the hat on the alphabet chart. "And the same thing happened when I wasn't sure how to spell the /r/ in *near*."

Link

Remind the students that they can use the alphabet chart as they write.

"You can do the same thing as I've done. You can use an alphabet chart to help you, and guess what? I have your very own alphabet charts for each of you to use when you go to your writing places."

There was burst of excitement. "I know, I know. I know it's exciting—but I can't let you go until you look ready." The students quickly straightened out, placing their hands in their laps with serious looks on their faces in the hopes of being the first one selected to go back to their seats and try out this new tool.

MID-WORKSHOP TEACHING POINT

Tell the story of a child who used the alphabet chart well.

"I was watching Perri write about her bird and she was trying to write *bird*. She forgot how to write the /d/ sound, so guess what, she did? She looked on the alphabet chart and thought, 'Which picture starts like the /d/ sound? Oh! *Duck* starts like the /d/ sound.' Then Perri wrote the letter *d* at the end of the word *bird*. So writers, you can find sounds for letters on the chart just like Perri did."

Leah spends much of her time writing fluently because she wants to demonstrate that the alphabet chart doesn't interrupt the flow of the writing, nor does it influence her work with every word.

This is not a usual active involvement. Leah merely calls on one student. This component of the minilesson gives Patrick a chance to be actively involved, but no one else. It's important for you to recognize that this isn't a usual sort of active involvement—but also to realize that all of us make exceptions some of the time.

As discussed in the introduction, you may choose to give students individual name charts or word walls instead of alphabet charts.

TIME TO CONFER

Be on the lookout for a child whose work can be used as an exemplar. Also look out for children who use the alphabet chart well because you'll want to celebrate this. Notice, too, those who rely too heavily on the chart either by using it for every letter or by copying words off the chart. If you find this happening, you may need more whole-class lessons, but it's more likely that you'll address these needs through individual conferences.

You are almost in the last part of this unit of study, so you'll definitely want to use your conferring checklist today to assess what children are doing or are almost doing, and to confer toward whatever feels just outside of a child's independent reach. Try to intervene today to teach strategies or habits that can soon become part of a child's independent repertoire.

 These conferences in *The Conferring Handbook* may be especially helpful today:

▶ *"What's the Story in This Picture?"*
▶ *"Where Is Your Writing?"*
▶ *"Let Me Show You How to Write More"*

Also, if you have *Conferring with Primary Writers*, you may want to refer to the conferences in part one.

AFTER-THE-WORKSHOP SHARE

When the class has gathered, ask them to practice using the alphabet chart once together, quickly.

"Writers, I saw so many of you using your alphabet charts today to help you. Let's practice that together right now on the rug. If you wanted to write about a wild-eyed goat but you weren't sure what letter makes the sound /g/ in *goat*, which section of your alphabet chart could help you? Read the pictures until you can find the one that might help you." The children eventually pointed to g. "And if you wanted to write about our window shade falling down and you weren't sure the letter to use at the start of *window*, point to the place on your alphabet chart where you could get help." They did.

Choose one child who has used an out-of-the-way letter to share. Ask children to use the alphabet chart to find the letter for this sound.

"When you use your alphabet chart, you can write anything! Listen to the cool things your friends are writing about."

"Chloe wrote this [*Fig. X-1*]: 'One day my mom came in the house. She looked like a *zombie*.' What a word! A zombie. Would you kids help each other and use your alphabet charts? See if you could start that word—*zombie*."

It's inevitable that some kids will not need to use the alphabet chart in order to know the letter at the start of goat. Focus your attention on the children who are finding the letter through reading the pictures on the chart, and make sure they have enough time to go through the process.

One day my mom came in the house. She looked like a zombie. She got a glass of milk and then she drank it. Then she went to bed in the middle of the morning. Can you believe that?
The end.

Fig. X-1 Chloe

▶ Once again, use the alphabet chart as you write in front of the class. This time, emphasize that you use the chart only for the trickiest parts, not for every word. "Remember yesterday I showed you how to use the alphabet chart? I want to remind you that writers just use the alphabet chart once in a while as they write, not for every word. Lots of words we can just write the best we can." Here, you could add onto yesterday's writing. You could stop at only one or two sounds and refer to the chart. You'd move quickly through the rest of the sentence and not use the chart. "See what I did. I used the chart only when I really needed it. For the sounds I thought I knew, I just wrote them down without stopping. I want to see all of you try this today with your writing! Off you go."

CREATING A PLACE FOR WRITING-IN-PROGRESS: LONG-TERM PROJECTS

GETTING READY

▶ Child's writing with sticky notes or taped or stapled paper pieces
▶ Student folders with red-dot stickers on the left pockets and green-dot stickers on the right pockets
▶ Your own writing—some finished and some not
▶ Your empty folder, appropriately dotted
▶ Stapler, tape, and/or sticky notes available in the writing center
⦿ See CD-ROM for resources

EARLIER, YOU TAUGHT CHILDREN THAT EVEN WHEN THEY THINK *they are finished, they can go back and work more. This is at the heart of teaching children to work in rigorous ways. As part of this, we need to teach children to plan that their work will take multiple days.*

The following three sessions all help writers write more. Today, you'll introduce a system that encourages children to work on pieces for a sequence of days: You'll teach them to tape or staple more paper onto the bottoms of their stories, to let these one-page stories become as long as Chinese dragons. After several days, you'll want to nudge children to approach writing with a plan to write in booklets of several pages, as we do in Session XII. Finally, in Session XIII, you'll encourage revisions.

Materials carry messages. At the start of this unit, we gave children blank paper, then we added a line for the writer's name and a line or two or three for the message. We did this knowing that changing the paper, in and of itself, could nudge children to change their expectations for their work. Today, we'll again use materials to convey a message. This time, the new materials will be just two sticker dots, a red one and a green one, for each child's two-pocket folder. These stickers create a system for differentiating finished (red-dot pocket) from ongoing work (green-dot pocket).

After today, children will see that they can add more paper to their pages, and when children store their work in their folders, they'll put finished work in the left pocket of their folder—behind the red dot—and ongoing work in the right pocket—behind the green dot.

The Minilesson

Connection

Tell the story of one child who realized she had more to say, stapled a paper tail onto her page for the rest of her words, and then stored her writing in a special place so she could come back to it tomorrow.

"The best thing happened yesterday. Lindsay wrote her story, look it says 'I'm on a motorboat. It went very fast.' *Then* she decided, 'Wait! I have to tell what happened next!' so she got another piece of paper and stapled it on like this." I held it up.

"This is *exactly* what grownup authors do! We add on! We say more! Our one-page stories grow . . . and grow . . . and grow!"

"But writers, what happened next is that I said, 'Put away your work. Time for share,' and Lindsay looked like this." I reenacted an oh-no-what-am-I-going-to-do-my-story-won't-grow-after-all look and shoved the piece into the folder. "But then Lindsay and I decided, 'No, she's not going to stop work on this story just because writing time is over!'"

Tell children that today you'll teach them a way to keep working on the same story for several days.

"So I want to show you what Lindsay did to keep working on her story—because I'm hoping we'll all do this."

Teaching

Show children the way one child uses dots to separate folder pockets for finished and for ongoing work.

"Look at Lindsay's folder. You know how traffic lights use a red light to say 'stop' and a green light to say 'go'? Lindsay decided to use these dots in her writing folder. This side of her folder is for finished—stopped—work. And look! Her motorboat story is over here, in the green side for 'go.' She is still working on this story."

Notice that in order to teach the process, I don't summarize the events but retell them, bit by bit. Notice also that I involve Lindsay in the actual carpentry of adding on. Instead of creating the longer papers ourselves, we need to tap into the special energy created when children staple pieces of paper together to make more room for their writing. Before long, you will distribute several-page-long booklets in the writing center, but meanwhile, for a few days, kids love the chance to literally construct longer stories.

In teaching writing, you'll find yourself repeating certain powerful phrases. During the first month of school, I find myself saying, "Your story is growing!" often.

Your children will be so thrilled to see their writing literally grow that another year, you may find yourself tempted to hurry into this phase. Don't do this. Postpone the day when children begin to construct 'the longest stories ever,' because when this comes just as energy in this unit has begun to wane, it can give your children a second wind.

Lindsay didn't come up with the idea of red and green dots alone; she had help inventing it, from me, the day before. It isn't unusual for us to take an idea we, or a child, invented years ago and act as if that day a child invented it. We do this to help children feel like they are coauthors of the community and to give the new policy social power.

Active Engagement

Recruit children to help you sort your writing similarly.

"Will you help me do this with my stack of writing? I'll tell you about the piece, and then you tell the person beside you if I should put it in the red-dot section," I pointed, "or the green-dot section."

"This is the piece I wrote about the wooden boat I made, and I already went back and added about how I had it in the park, and I put more details in my drawing. Tell the person beside you if you think this should go in the green section or in the red section."

"This is a story I started with a few of you about my baby rabbits, but I didn't tell that I had ten of them, and I gave them all away. Tell your partner where you think this story should go."

"This is a story I wrote about when I got an ice cream from the ice cream truck. But I didn't tell that as soon as the man gave it to me, I took one lick, and all of the ice cream fell off the cone and plopped onto the street! Tell your partner where you think it belongs."

"What I heard you kids saying is that I have more work to do on two of my stories and you are right. So that's what I'll do today."

Link

Tell children that today they'll need to sort their writing into categories: finished or ongoing writing.

"Today, let's put our pieces in either the red section of our folders if the work is finished, stopped, work or in the green section if the work that is still ongoing. So today, before you write, you will need to go through your stack of writing from the start of the year and look at each piece and decide, 'Is this stopped? Is this ongoing?'"

"Today, writers, when you get your folders you'll see all your work is in a pile in the middle (not in the pockets) and you'll see you have a red-dot stop pocket and a green-dot keep-going pocket, like Lindsay. The first thing to do today is to go through your writing like I've just done and to divide it into the two piles—one for finished, stopped, work and one for ongoing work. Okay, writers?"

We say, "Tell the person beside you," because then more children are actually engaged, doing the work. Calling on one or two children is not active engagement for all.

Although my explicit goal is to teach children how to use red and green dots to categorize work as "finished" or "ongoing," I'm meanwhile reminding children of the importance of writing stories that contain details, and of the fact that writers revise by telling more.

This could serve as the active engagement phase of the minilesson, but it entails a whole class of children spreading out the contents of their folders, all while sitting squashed on the carpet. We're apt to do this with older children, but for kindergartners it's too complicated in the midst of a minilesson.

TIME TO CONFER

At the start of the writing workshop, you'll want to refrain from conferring for just long enough to let all the children settle into their work. This gives them a few minutes to initiate some work and it gives you an opportunity to study the patterns in the class without targeting your attention on any one child yet. After a bit, you'll pull alongside a writer as he or she works. Get into the habit of first listening and watching without intervening. You don't want every child to learn to stop work whenever you draw close! Then you can intervene. In this session, your conferring will involve lots of conferences—see "What's Happening in Your Piece?" in the *Conferring with Primary Writers* book geared toward helping children say more—and then your conferring will involve teaching about stapling to add a second or third page.

These conferences in *The Conferring Handbook* may be especially helpful today:

▶ *"What's the Story in This Picture?"*
▶ *"Where Is Your Writing?"*
▶ *"Let Me Show You How to Write More"*

Also, if you have *Conferring with Primary Writers*, you may want to refer to the following conference:

▶ **"What's Happening in Your Piece?"**

AFTER-THE-WORKSHOP SHARE

Before children gather on the rug, show them how you filed your current writing in the appropriate pocket of your folder.

"It's time for writing to end. Before you come to the rug, watch me. See what I do." Role-playing, I said, "Hmmm. I'm trying to think if I'm done with this piece or if I want to keep working on it. Let's see. I think it's keep-going work." I pointed to the green sticker. "It's green light work, not stopped work. I have more to add to the piece so I'm going to put it here, on this (the right) side of my folder."

Ask children to file their work in the appropriate pocket of their own folders.

"Will each of you look at the work you are doing and decide where you, as a writer, need to store that work? After that, will you bring your folders to the rug?"

Offer students the story of how one child filed her work today.

"I wanted to share how Allison used her folder today. She was writing this story," I hold it up, "about her bag breaking. First, her mom didn't fix it. Allison didn't have time today to end her story by saying her mom finally fixed it, so Allison put her story on the green side—the green, still-going side. That was smart work, Allison."

Let children talk over their filing decisions of today with a partner.

"At the end of every writing time, you need to decide where you want to put your piece. Will you each show the person beside you where you put today's work, and tell that person why you made that decision?"

Throughout these units, we often suggest you ask your students to do something rather than tell them to do something. Some students know that asking can be a polite way of telling, and some students may take your question literally and believe they can choose whether to do as you ask. These students may need you to either tell them to do something using very direct terms or else to explain that when you ask, you don't mean that this is optional—you are using questions as a means to suggest (or to tell).

- Tell the story of how a child decided on which side of his folder his writing should go. You could give two examples, one of a red dot side and one green. "Yasir, could you tell us why this piece is on the red side? And could you tell us why this piece is on the green side." After Yasir explains, you could say, "Great. It was so smart of Yasir to decide to put the writing about his dog on the red side, since he does not know what else to add. And he wants to write more words, like authors do, in his baseball piece so he put that under the green dot. I love it. Good decision! Let's all check our folders. Is the writing we are going to work on today on the green side? Knowing this should help us all get to work right away. I'm going to watch and see how quickly we can get to our writing."

- "Writers, I was so excited yesterday. During choice time, Sasha and Talia were making a barn and first they made it in a quick fashion—just a square for horses. But then they looked at it and said, 'Wait! We should have a place for the saddles and the hay—a place where the horses can't go!' They added that. Then they got the idea to make different stalls for different horses. But the sad thing was it was time for lunch. Then, they got the idea—to put a green dot on a paper and leave it here beside their barn as a 'still-working-on-this' message to the rest of us. And today during choice time they went back to their barn. I know that yesterday, at the end of writing time, some of you did the same thing—you put your writing in the still-working-on-it section. Thumbs up if you did that!"

- "I was looking at your precious writing last weekend, and I saw some of you had jammed your writing into your folder like this and it was all scrunched up!" You could then talk about how to use your hands to straighten your pieces of writing into a neat pack and then slide them into the pocket.

INTRODUCING BOOKLETS

GETTING READY

- Trays full of ready-made little booklets made from 3-4 sheets of paper stapled together (you'll want to make several booklets, each using whatever kinds of paper your children have been using)
- Ready-made large booklet for your demonstration, marker
- Picture book well known to the class
- See CD-ROM for resources

TEACHERS OFTEN SAY TO US, "I DON'T KNOW HOW *you think of your minilessons. Where do you get the ideas?" There are a few answers. One is that ideas come from a general sense for the journey we anticipate the class taking across the month (and that comes from prior experiences with other classes). The second idea is that we get ideas for minilessons from our colleagues. When a grade level is working within the same unit of study, we often devote grade level meetings to swapping ideas for minilessons, and the conversations are full of comments like, "I tried your minilesson about . . . only I tweaked it a little so that. . . ." We also get ideas for minilesson from professional books. And finally, we get ideas for minilessons from the conferring we do with individual children. The idea for this minilesson came from conferences, and the goal is for more children to learn they can approach a new piece of writing by planning to write it as a book in which the story is carried across pages. Most first graders (and some kindergartners) are able to write sentences under the pictures.*

For many children, it takes a while to learn to tell a story in small increments. It's common for the first page of a story to summarize the event ("I went to the game. My team won."). Other pages become add-ons prolonging the final page ("We went home on the subway. I went to bed.") or they journey back to the start of the event ("I had a coke.").

This session will help children plan for and write a book that spans several pages.

The Minilesson

Connection

Tell writers that today they'll go from writing one-page stories to writing in books.

"Writers, I am so excited about our writing workshop! Today we're ready to take a big step ahead. Most of us have been writing our stories on one page. Well, when we read stories in books, there is almost always more than one page! Today, you are going to start to write your stories in books that are like those that other authors write!"

Teaching

Point out that a picture book doesn't have a summary but instead has a detailed story that spans pages.

"Yesterday in the read-aloud, we read Dav Pilkey's book, *The Paperboy*. Dav could have written his story on one paper." I showed a summary of the book on chart paper:

The paperboy wakes up and he delivers his papers and then comes home.

"But Dav decided to write his story as a whole book. So on this page," I opened to the first page, "the boy is still sleeping." I turned the page. "The next page doesn't say," I said the upcoming words in a rush, "'then he delivers the paper and comes home.' Instead, this page shows him getting out of bed." I turned to the next page. "And going down the stairs," I turned the next page, "and eating breakfast," I turned the next page, "and filling his bag with newspapers. . . ."

How children thrive on the simple fact that you refer to them as writers, and liken their work to that which is done by published authors.

It's important to choose a picture book that doesn't have a lot of lines of words on each page. Published authors make the best mentors when their work feels attainable on some level to the young writers.

Explain to the children that they can write detailed stories that span pages also.

"I'm telling you this because you kids can do the exact same thing! You can stretch your stories out and tell them across a lot of pages."

Active Engagement

Remind the children of an experience the class has had, and offer a too-short summary.

"Let's say you wanted to write a book about when Mr. Kolk, the librarian, came and showed us three great new books. Would page one be 'Mr. Kolk told us about three books, and then he left. It was fun.'?"

"Nooo."

Ask the children to turn to a neighbor and offer the first page of a several page story.

"Tell a friend what you might write on page one—just page one—in a book about Mr. Kolk coming to our classroom and showing those books."

Share with the class several children's first pages—ones with an appropriate start.

"I heard Victoria saying she could start, 'Yesterday Mr. Kolk knocked on our door. We said, 'Come in.'"

"And Joe said the story could start, 'Mr. Kolk talked to us. He showed us *The Tenth Good Thing About Barney*.'"

"These beginnings are both smart work. You are both doing what Dav does in *The Paperboy*. He doesn't start his story saying, 'The paperboy delivers papers.' He starts it:

"The mornings of the paperboy are still dark and they are always cold, even in summer."

Link

Ask the children to write on the new paper—the blank booklets with several pages.

"So writers, if you are starting a new story today—would you get a book with lots of pages? And will you think out how the story will go? Try different beginnings in your mind because you'll want a beginning that doesn't give everything away."

This is another common teaching pattern for a minilesson to take—show children a published author's work, point out what that author has done that the children might try, and ask them to have a go at it for themselves.

If you suspect that children will find this beginning to be perfectly acceptable, don't ask for their opinion. Instead, give your own opinion, explain why the first opening won't work, and offer a better first page. Then have children help you imagine what might be written on the second page.

Though you aren't telling children to focus on using details, by asking them to spread the same story out over more pages, you are asking them to go into more depth than they would normally—in essence, asking them to write with more detail. It's important that you don't give the children the impression that you are asking only and exclusively for longer stories.

TIME TO CONFER

Often your conferences help children to use the concepts and strategies you teach in minilessons. This is important, because you want your teaching to make a difference in children's work. I often tell principals, for example, that one way to supervise a writing workshop is to look at what children are doing and say, "What evidence do I see that the teacher has been teaching something?" Your conferences can make it much more likely that children apply to their writing what you taught in the minilesson. In this conference, try conferring with *The Paperboy* (or whichever book you used in the minilesson) under your arm. Say to children, "What you've done, which is a lot like Dav Pilkey did, is . . ." or "You might want to try what another author did. Look how Dav Pilkey. . . ."

Use these references to nudge children to write across pages, to work on their lead, to record words, to add details — or anything else!

If all you accomplish is that you help some children assume the identity of being an author, your time was well spent.

These conferences in *The Conferring Handbook* may be especially helpful today:

▶ *"What's the Story in This Picture?"*
▶ *"Where Is Your Writing?"*
▶ *"Let Me Show You How to Write More"*

Also, if you have *Conferring with Primary Writers*, you may want to refer to the conferences in part one.

After-the-Workshop Share

Gather children and let them share their work with a partner.

"Writers, would you kids sit with a friend and read your beautiful long books to each other? I am so excited by what you are doing!"

Ask one writer who has taken the idea of the minilesson to heart—in this case, one who has written a lot—to share.

"Let me share with you some of the amazing things you kids have done. Sean, tell us what you did today."

"Today I wrote about the day I had my best soccer game. I listened and wrote down the sounds and guess what? I have a looong story."

Point out to the children what the student did that you hope they will learn to do. Tell students they can do the same.

"Writers, do you see what happened [*Fig. XII-1*]? Sean wrote a story with a lot of pages, he didn't just tell it all at once. We were so lucky he did that because we learned so much about the day he had his best soccer game. We learned he played five games in one day. We also learned that he got six points. We even learned that he had to move to a different spot! You can do the same as Sean—you can write a story that goes for a bunch of pages and not tell the whole thing all at once."

My best soccer game
I played today five soccer games.
Then we won one game and I got
six points.
Then I moved to a different spot.
Then I won the game and I went
home.

Fig. XII-1   Sean

Getting a lot on the paper is addressed in future minilessons. Occasionally, you might use the share, as I do here, to briefly introduce what will be taught in detail in future minilessons.

IF CHILDREN NEED MORE TIME

▸ Teach the children the strategy of touching each page and telling aloud the story that will go on that page. This reinforces the idea that writers stretch stories out across pages.

▸ You could teach a minilesson about the conventions of books. For example, you might say, "Writers, may I stop all of you? Now that you are writing in books, one thing you'll need to do is to add page numbers to your pages. Usually they go here, the lower right corner. As you count your pages, write the number on that page. Skip the cover though, because books never have page numbers on their covers."

▸ You could show children that sometimes you look back over pieces you've written and decide they deserve to be whole books. You could read aloud a piece which was originally one page and show children how you rewrote it in a bit-by-bit fashion across many pages.

WIDENING WRITING POSSIBILITIES: LISTS AND LETTERS

GETTING READY

▶ Several pieces of your own writing—in different genres, on different paper
▶ Two or three new kinds of paper to help children imagine writing in a new genre
● See CD-ROM for resources

YOUR STUDENTS AT THIS POINT WILL BE WRITING STORIES *from their lives, drawing the pictures and writing the words as best as they can. The workshop probably has begun to settle down a bit. It feels to you as if most children have an idea for what to do during writing. You now have a decision to make. Do you want to continue to emphasize that writers tell true stories from their lives, or do you want to introduce the idea that people write for lots of reasons and in lots of genres? There is no right or wrong answer to this question. The curriculum we lay out for the next few months spotlights the primacy of narrative, and in future books we'll explain this decision. It won't be until February that we describe a sequence of units designed to help children write non-narratives. So you may want to make space during the next a few days for children to write in a whole range of genre.*

This minilesson will invite children to write in a range of genres, for a range of purposes.

THE MINILESSON

Connection

Remind writers that they've been thinking up topics and writing true stories. Tell them there are more kinds of writing than just stories.

"Writers, so far this year you've been writing true stories. But of course there are lots of kinds of writing in the world. When I care about a topic, I sometimes write more than one kind of writing about that topic, and you can do that, too."

Teaching

Tell writers that when you love a topic, you write lots of kinds of writing related to the topic. Show examples, naming the genre.

"You know that one topic I love to write about is running. I have already written a bunch of running stories. Instead of writing a brand-new story, I am going to write about running in brand-new ways. May I show you what is inside my writing folder?"

Leah slowly opened the folder, knowing that simply by being slow and dramatic she can create excitement and keep her young students engaged and interested during the minilesson. "Well, my first piece is a list of all the things I need when I run. May I show it to you?"

"It says, 'Things you need when you run.' First I list sneakers, then shorts, then a water bottle. Do you see how I took something I love—like running—and I made a list?"

"May I show you something else? I wrote a letter to my friend asking her if she would run with me this afternoon. May I read it to you? 'Dear Jane, The marathon is coming up soon. I know I am not running enough. Maybe if I ran with you, I would run more. Do you think that might work for you? Do you want to run together on Tuesday? Write and let me know. Love, Leah.' Do you see how I took a topic I care about and made a letter about my topic?"

Don't offer more than one or two new choices because your children won't be writing in lots of genres for long at this point. Save stationery for letters and paper for poetry for later in the year so it will be fresh.

Leah is wise to store her writing inside a folder that resembles her children's folders. Leah can confer with this folder in her hand.

The writing which Leah uses on her demonstration is sparse. She gains nothing by showing children longer and more lavish pieces.

"Aren't all those genres a lot to introduce at once?" some of you might be thinking. If the purpose of this lesson was to teach students how to write a good letter or a well-organized list, then you'd certainly be teaching too much. But the purpose of this lesson is to teach students that they can go back and write about topics more than once, and that they can do so in a range of genres.

Tell children they, too, can write in many genres.

"I'm telling you about this because you can do the exact same thing! You can take topics that you have already written about and write lists or letters or anything else about those same topics."

Active Engagement

Ask children to think of a topic they care about. What else could they write related to that topic? Ask for them to share this with a friend.

"Take a moment now and think about a topic that is important to you. Think, 'What else could I write on my topic?'"

The students closed their eyes for a moment. "Okay, now open your eyes and tell your friend what your topic might be and the kind of writing you might try."

Link

Send children off to do all these kinds of writing.

"I can't wait to see what you write today. Writers, thumbs up if you are ready to write. Okay, off you go."

Remember that this can be your mantra. "I'm telling you this because you can do the exact same thing." Say this— and other phrases—often enough that they become ingrained in children's minds.

TIME TO CONFER

In this session, your conferences will help children notice reasons to write, and you'll encourage children to write in a variety of genres to accomplish a range of purposes. You may want to try the following:

▶ Refer to writing that is around you in the room. "Do you see how I've listed what we plan to do today in school? Some kids like to list what they plan to do at home." "Earlier today, I wrote myself a reminder note. Writers do that if they want to remember something. Why don't you. . . ."

▶ Review with a child the writing that he or she has done so far in the year. "What I notice is that you've done lots of writing that goes like this: (_____). You might want to try some different kinds of writing. May I give you a few ideas and see if one sounds good?"

 These conferences in *The Conferring Handbook* may be especially helpful today:

▶ "What's the Story in This Picture?"
▶ "Where Is Your Writing?"
▶ "Let Me Show You How to Write More"

Also, if you have *Conferring with Primary Writers*, you may want to refer to the conferences in part one.

After-the-Workshop Share

Choose some children who have taken the advice of the minilesson, children who have written pieces in a new genre, to share.

"Writers, let's share some of the types of writing you did today. Robert, will you share?" Robert told the class that he wanted his uncle Scott to teach him some new tricks, so he wrote him a letter and was going to mail it to him that day. [*Fig. XIII-1*]

Kenya shared her sign. [*Fig. XIII-2*]

"A sign! What other signs do we need in this school?" wondered Leah.

Brianna shared her letter. Leah added, "Wow, so you wrote a letter to someone in the class to put in her cubby? Wow, I bet a lot of us have ideas for letters we'd want to write to each other!"

When Annie [*Fig. XIII-3*] shared her list of songs from music class, children noticed that Annie had written a story also about singing a song with her mom. They talked about how one topic led to lots of kinds of writing.

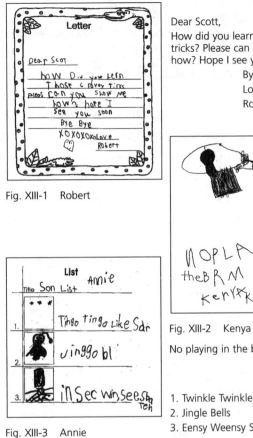

Fig. XIII-1   Robert

Dear Scott,
How did you learn those groovy tricks? Please can you show me how? Hope I see you soon.
Bye, bye.
Love,
Robert

Fig. XIII-2   Kenya

No playing in the bathroom.

Fig. XIII-3   Annie

1. Twinkle Twinkle Little Star
2. Jingle Bells
3. Eensy Weensy Spider

Leah wants students to realize that topics aren't used up if they have been written about one time. Students often do some of their best writing on topics they come back to again and again.

IF CHILDREN NEED MORE TIME

You could teach variations of the preceding minilesson. (However, an entire unit of study on this topic comes later in the year, so you may decide not to elaborate a great deal on it now.)

▸ Take a class topic and show the class that you could write about that topic in many ways. For example, you could take the topic of the class snail and make a list of foods snails eat or write a letter to the pet shop thanking the owner for the snail.

▸ You could pull children together and tell them, "You are all authors. Today we're going to do what authors do. Let me tell you about one author." Then you might introduce an author, such as Tomie de Paola, who has written lots of different kinds of things. You could hold up *The Popcorn Book* or *The Cloud Book*, showing that he makes lots of different kinds of writing. Then you could suggest that children in the room can write any of these kinds of writing.

▸ You could begin by talking about purposes we have for writing. "I had a party for my grandma and I realized there's a lot of writing to do for a party! I wrote a list of who would come and a shopping list. I wrote plans for the party. I made a card for my grandma."

▸ You could put paper in the choice centers throughout your classroom—the block center, the dramatic play center, the art center—and encourage children to write a phone message by the telephone, a shopping list by the refrigerator, a recipe by the cooking center, a play by the puppetry center, a story in the library.

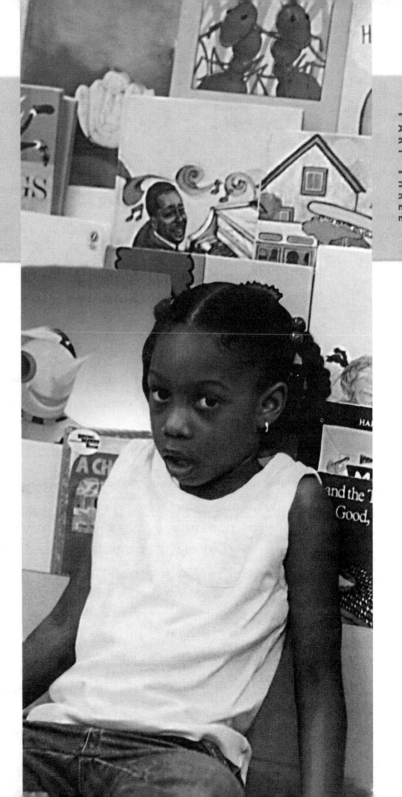

WIDENING WRITING POSSIBILITIES: REAL-WORLD PURPOSES

GETTING READY

▶ Several pieces of your own writing of various genres necessitated by everyday life, on chart paper or projected from a transparency

● See CD-ROM for resources

IN THE PREVIOUS SESSION, YOU SHOWED CHILDREN *that when writers have topics they care about, they often write several pieces on that topic, each in a different genre for a different purpose related to that topic. Today you'll revisit the idea of writing in lots of forms for lots of reasons. But instead of suggesting this originate with a favorite topic such as running, you'll suggest that writers write for real-world purposes.*

Today, then, you'll help children realize that during every section of the room and part of the day, there are reasons to write—and you'll invite children to do that writing.

THE MINILESSON

Connection

Tell children that in the same way that certain topics make us want to do all kinds of writing, our daily life can make us want to do all kinds of writing too.

"Writers, yesterday we talked about how a really good topic for writing often gets us going on a lot of pieces of writing. And I saw Jeremy go back to his story about visiting his grandma and write a thank you letter to her, which was so smart."

"Today I want to tell you about another kind of thinking that makes me really want to write. What I do is I think about the things I'm already doing today and I think, 'Could writing help me do any of those better?'"

Tell children what you will talk about today: finding writing projects in daily life.

"I'll show you how this helps me come up with writing projects for myself."

Teaching

Explain how life presents instances that call for writing.

"Today, for example, I came into the class early and I thought, 'I need to remember my plans for the day—you know, what will we do first and next. So I thought, 'Hey—I could write my plans, and I did, right here." Leah quickly showed them on the overhead.

"Then I realized we need more books and I wasn't sure if the library has them. And I thought, 'Hey, I could write a letter and find out.'" Leah showed them the letter. "Then I thought, 'I better do something nice for my mother's birthday.' And I thought, 'I could make her a book with memories in it.'" Leah showed them the little book she'd made.

When we teach children writing strategies, we can also work in other lessons. For example, Leah is teaching children that they can become famous for the good work they do. She's also teaching children that writers take pleasure in generating projects for themselves.

Leah decides to put her list on the overhead so that all the children can see it. The other examples aren't enlarged, so Leah just holds them up so the students can see.

Active Engagement

Tell students about an incident in the life of a student in the class, and ask them to tell a partner what kind of writing seems called for there.

"So I want you to try this out. Before school, I asked Nicole what she's been doing for fun and she said she's learning different yo-yo tricks. Tell your partner what writing Nicole might want to do."

The room erupted into chatter. Children mentioned lists of tricks, books of directions, and an invitation to a parent who could show the class more tricks.

If the students don't have many ideas on their own yet, you may want to make some suggestions. Students need to see that any one instance has many possible related writing projects.

If your students seem to need another try, give them another daily event to think about with their partner.

"Bradley told me he is hoping to convince his dad to take him to the Baseball Hall of Fame. Tell your partner how this might give Bradley a reason to write. What might *he* write?"

You might have some children share their ideas with the class to help everyone understand the kinds of writing projects that can come of any event.

Ask students to think about their own lives and what writing projects are called for in them. Wait until they seem to have ideas.

"Before you go, would you think about what *you* have been doing in your life and think, 'How could writing help me with that?' If you get an idea, thumbs up."

The ritual of "thumbs up" is an alternative to calling for a show of hands. This is a less in-your-face way to signal to each other. It's a widely used ritual in the classrooms we know best.

Link

Let students begin writing life-inspired projects.

"Okay writers, lots of you seem like you are dying to write from what is happening in your life. Get started."

TOURO COLLEGE LIBRARY

If your children are writing functional writing—signs, labels, notes, letters, cards, and the like—this gives you lots of reasons to argue that the child needs to really listen for and record sounds or others won't be able to read it.

You can then continue with work you did earlier as you help children listen for and distinguish sounds, attach them to letters, record the letters, and so on.

Encourage children to reread often as they write. Remember that if you know what a child intended to say and you know also that the child hasn't recorded enough clues that he or she (or you) will be able to decipher the message on another day, you can scrawl a tiny cursive translation along the edge of the paper so that on another day, you can feign being able to read the child's text.

 These conferences in *The Conferring Handbook* may be especially helpful today:

▶ *"What's the Story in This Picture?"*
▶ *"Where Is Your Writing?"*
▶ *"Let Me Show You How to Write More"*

Also, if you have *Conferring with Primary Writers*, you may want to refer to the conferences in part one.

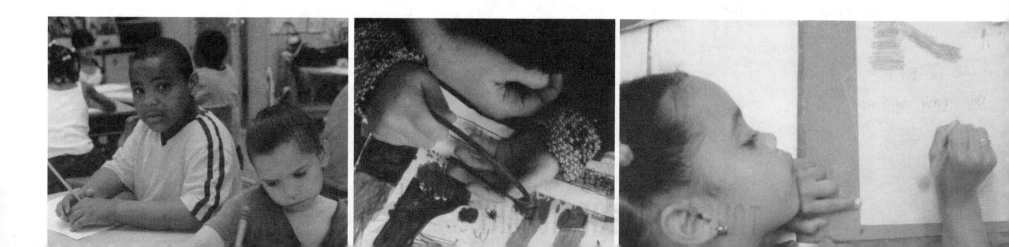

AFTER-THE-WORKSHOP SHARE

In preparation for the next part of the unit, demonstrate for students how you choose a piece of writing to publish.

"After we've been writing for a while, writers choose a piece we love, one we are absolutely crazy about, and we publish it. We put it in the library or read it aloud to our friends. So today, we're going to reread everything we've written and choose one piece we especially love, and then fix it up for publication."

Leah took out the contents of her folder. She laid one piece after another around her until she was surrounded by a web of pieces. "I'm trying to decide which one of these to put in the library." After a moment, she picked up one story and said, "I think people will really like this one." She chose one about art class being cancelled.

Highlight for students what you hope they noticed about your demonstration. Review how writers pick pieces of writing to publish.

"Did you see that I looked back over all my writing and chose one I thought readers would like? I had to spread out all my pieces and remember them all. I had to reread some of them."

Ask students to follow your example and choose a piece of writing to work on and to publish at the end of the unit.

"Would each of you, right now, go through your folders and choose a piece that you want to fix up and fancy up for publication? We'll work with them tomorrow. Put it right on top of your folder."

Get students ready to pick up tomorrow where they left off today.

"Good job. Now, think for a minute about how you can add to this writing. Whisper to a partner the first thing you are going to add when you work tomorrow. Great!"

We act as if our children will be absolutely crazy about pieces of writing. We assume they'll love writing as we do. In this way, we help children take on the roles of being avid writers.

A demonstration alone isn't usually explicit enough to do the job.

You may want to ask students to help one another do this so that they choose pieces with other listeners in mind.

FIXING UP WRITING

GETTING READY

▶ A bare-bones story of an event the class has experienced together, written on chart paper
▶ Marker
● See CD-ROM for resources

IN THIS, THE FIRST UNIT OF YOUR WRITING WORKSHOP, *it is especially important to induct each child into the identity and life of being an author. Publishing one's writing is an absolutely crucial part of this, and it's especially important now when you are helping children learn what writing is for and why it merits so much hard and loving work. Today, you'll tell your students that writers send work out into the world, that we write for real readers. Writers don't publish everything they write—we look through it, choose our best, and then make our best better.*

There are lots of ways to publish student work. You can bind it into small booklets, make cassettes full of children reading their stories aloud, invite parents or other classes in to celebrate, have readings on stage in the auditorium complete with the PA system. Our suggestion, however, is to imagine gradient of publication methods and to be sure this first publication is as simple as it can be. That way, over the course of time, things can gradually escalate, and you won't find yourself needing to unroll the red carpet every time.

You'll want to expect less fixing up and fancying up at this stage, too. Whereas eventually you may ask children to write "about the author" sections and dedication pages, for now, we suggest that fixing up involves adding to the picture and the words, and fancying up means adding a cover or a bit of color (of course, any child can surprise you by doing more).

In this session, you will teach children that writers fix up their work and revise it so it says everything they mean it to say before it's sent out in the world.

The Minilesson

Connection

Tell students that writers do all they have been doing—and that writers publish their writing.

"Writers, since school began, you all have been doing just what writers do. Writers think of ideas to write, they plan their writing, they pick paper to match their plans, and they write as best they can and keep going. But yesterday we learned writers *also* publish their work, and today I'll show you how to do that because in a few days we need to be ready for a publishing party."

Teaching

Remind children that when it is time to publish, a writer looks over everything he or she has written and chooses one text to fix up and fancy up.

"All through this school and all across the world, when writers know that it will soon be time to publish, the writer rereads what he or she has written and chooses the best, saying, 'This is the piece I'm going to publish.' We did that yesterday. Then, writers get the piece ready to go out in the world."

"Have you ever seen a person getting ready to be married, or to graduate, or to go to a show, or to a birthday? Usually the person fancies himself or herself up. The same happens with writing."

"Before writers send our writing out for real, true readers to read it, we fix it up and then we fancy it up."

As the unit draws toward a conclusion, this is a good time to name what children have learned to do. I essentially say, "Writers do all these things . . . and you have done them also!"

I do two things to make this minilesson memorable. First, I use a metaphor that may be memorable for some children. They're getting their pieces ready to go out in the world just like people get ready to be married or go to a party. And the phrase "fix up and fancy up" has the rhythm and alliteration to make it stick. I continue to use this phrase throughout the year.

Active Engagement

Ask children to help you fix up—revise—a story you've written about an event the class knows well.

"So I was hoping you'd help me fix up my story. I'll read it and would you think, 'Does this make sense? How can Lucy fix it? What does Lucy need to add to have it say everything she means?' Here's the story."

Yesterday when we got to art, no one was. So we came back. We had free time.

"Would you tell the person beside you if you have ideas for how I could fix up my story?"

The children talked together. After a minute, I called on a few.

Noreen: "You left out a word. You gotta say, 'No one was *there.'*"

Zane: "You should tell why. Tell how she had a baby!"

"These are great ideas. So before I can publish my piece, I'll add the missing word and I'll reread what I've written and see if I can fit that other stuff in, too. Thanks a ton!"

Link

Let the students know they can try to revise their own writing today.

"So writers, today you'll take the piece you decided to publish and you'll reread it and fix it up. Ask, 'Does this make sense?' 'How can I fix it?' 'What can I add?'"

Notice again that I deliberately produce a tiny story, one that is easily improved, because my point is to show children how a writer rereads and revises. I wouldn't gain anything if the piece was longer and more elaborate. Notice also that I've written a story about a moment the class experienced together. This makes it easier for the children to imagine revisions.

TIME TO CONFER

Many of your conferences in this session will need to support revision. The easiest way to do this is to read the child's writing ("I love my rabbit. He kisses me.") and then to say back what the child has said as if it's the most interesting story in the world. "Wow! You really love that rabbit! He kisses you?" Most children will respond by saying more. Listen for a minute — then say that back too, asking, "Where will you add that?" as if, of course, this vital information needs to go in the writing. As the child revises by adding on, make a fuss about how this is what professional writers do. Remember as you confer that revision is a compliment for good work, not a way to repair inadequate work. If a child hesitates to revise, reveal your attitude toward revision by saying, "But this is such a great story. It deserves to be revised, to be made even better!" See the conferences cited at right in the *Conferring with Primary Writers book*.

Use your conferring chart to help you remember all the ways in which you could confer.

These conferences in *The Conferring Handbook* may be especially helpful today:

▶ *"What's the Story in This Picture?"*
▶ *"Where Is Your Writing?"*
▶ *"Let Me Show You How to Write More"*

Also, if you have *Conferring with Primary Writers*, you may want to refer to the following conferences:

▶ "What's Happening in Your Piece?"
▶ "Is This a Story About Your Life?"

After-the-Workshop Share

Select some pieces of student writing to share with the class. The pieces should demonstrate what you hope the children will all try to do.

"Writers, will you bring your piece with you and come to the carpet? Let me show you the smart ways in which you all have been fixing up your writing. Derrick decided he wanted to publish his story about his gerbils. [*Fig. XV-1*] He looked back over it and saw that he had writing on the first page," I showed it, not pointing out that the writing consisted of random strings of letters, "but he hadn't written anything on the other page! So he added more writing. On the last page, he wrote about his gerbils taking a nap."

"And Margay [*Fig. XV-2*] had decided to publish a piece she wrote on the very first day. Do you remember it? It went, 'I can read. I can write. I can spell.' Well, she decided that it was too short and that she should turn it into a book, so she named the book *Myself* and she added this page."

"Annabel has written about camping with her dad but she decided she wanted to add on that she and her dad came home, so she took out the staples in her book and added a page right in the middle, then stapled it back together again."

Remind children that they too can try these kinds of revision.

"Now, think to yourself which of the things these writers did would you like to try? Tell the person next to you what you might try tomorrow."

Make sure at least one of the examples you choose is something that you believe everyone can do at this stage. Don't showcase only the most advanced pieces of writing.

Fig. XV-1   Derrick

Myself I am special. What is special about you? I am special because I love myself.

Fig. XV-2   Margay

▸ "Often when writers revise their work they revise the words, just like we have been doing. I am so happy to see so many of you working to add more to your writing. I wanted to share another way that writers revise. Sometimes they also look at their drawings and say, 'What else could I add to make it even better?' and they add a detail to the drawing. Sarah did that the other day. Look at what she added. You can try that too."

▸ "Lots of you have been adding on to your writing to make it even better. Some of you found that you needed an extra piece of paper to add on to the end. I am so glad to see that. I noticed that a few of you wanted to add on to the middle part of your writing and you tried to squeeze in the words really tiny. I want to show you something else you can do if you want to add on to the middle." Gesture to a piece on the easel. "Here is the piece I have been working on." You read it. "I wanted to add on to this part here, but I don't have any more room. So, look what I can do. I can take this piece of paper, cut the bottom part off and tape the lines to the bottom of my piece. Then, I can add whatever words I want. If you think this would help you today, please raise your hand. Okay, you folks stay here on the rug and I will help you get the paper you need. When we come back together, we will see how these children revised their writing."

EDITING AND FANCYING UP WRITING

GETTING READY

- Piece of writing to publish, rewritten on chart paper with several misspellings of common sight words
- Picture to go with it
- Marker
- Second piece of writing with misspelled sight words
- Colored pencils for yourself and for each table of students
- See CD-ROM for resources

TEACHING EDITING IS HARD! *We often wonder where to start with our youngest writers. Should we teach them how to spell sight words correctly or to put spaces between words? Should we teach them to put more letters in their words or to add punctuation? The possibilities are endless. One place to begin is to teach children that writers reread their writing.*

Often students reread their writing quickly, glancing over their words in a sweep and declaring they are done. In this lesson, we teach students to reread carefully, pointing underneath each word. It is valuable for children to approximate this work even if their spellings are abbreviated and their reading skills emergent. At the very least, this helps children understand that their writing is potential reading material. Ideally children read noticing what readers need for the piece to make sense.

The students have worked hard. They have collected stories in their folders, chosen a story they wanted to work more on, and revised and edited that story. The final step is to make sure that the students spend time making their work look beautiful. You want students to understand that finished products look nice. Also, the process of "fancying up" their work makes students excited to present their work to an audience.

In today's lesson, you will teach students how to reread, check, and fix their writing. Then, mid-workshop, you will teach them to fancy up their work by adding details with colored pencils.

THE MINILESSON

Connection

Remind students of the process they have gone through up until now, and let them know they will be learning how to edit their writing.

"Writers, today we're going to fix up our writing in another way. Today we will edit our writing (that's what writers call it). Can you say that word: *edit*? When we edit our writing, we check everything to make sure people can read it."

Children will remember more when they are active. Even when they just voice the word—edit—they are being active.

Teaching

Edit your own writing in front of your children. Slow down your demonstration so the students can see the kinds of strategies you use.

"Today I am going to edit my own writing, and I want you to watch how I reread my writing, making sure that my words look right."

"Well, I better get my finger underneath my words so I can look at each word carefully." After Leah read along, she came to a misspelled word. "Hmmm— that word doesn't look right." She had spelled *went* as *wnt*. "Let me try and make that word look right." She wrote the correct spelling of *went* above *wnt*. Leah continued to read with her finger underneath the words. She stopped one more time, questioning whether her word looked right and then making a change above it.

"So writers, what did you notice I did to make sure my words looked right?"

"You read it all over again using your finger," Khadija said.

"You're right, Khadija, I did read my writing using my finger."

"Just like in reading!" Sam yelled out, "I use my finger in reading."

"You're right Sam, some of us put a finger underneath the words in reading."

"What else did I do? Did you notice that I checked to make sure my words looked right, and, if they didn't, I tried them again?"

Leah does not erase her spelling but rather crosses the word out with a single line and writes above it. This is something that she hopes the students will do. This allows the students' changes to be visible and lets Leah know the kinds of editing changes that each student does.

Leah doesn't find lots of words that require work. She doesn't want to demonstrate an editing process that is too ponderous. And she doesn't try to tuck lessons about punctuating and spelling into this broader lesson.

Active Engagement

Invite the children to join you in doing the same thing you have just done with a new story.

"So let's try that again, together, with this story." Leah showed the second story on chart paper. "I'll put my finger under the words and read it, and you tell your partner if the word looks right or if you'd change it. Then, after we have read the whole story, I'll ask for your suggestions." They did this.

Link

Ask the student to try this same thing, to try editing their own work by making sure their words look right.

"So writers, look again at the writing you will be publishing at our celebration tomorrow. Reread it like it was your independent reading book. Read it with your finger just like I did and check to make sure your words look right. And when there is a word that doesn't look right, rewrite it above so that it *does* look right. Okay?"

MID-WORKSHOP TEACHING POINT

Let the students know that they are getting their pieces ready for an audience.

"I can't believe how hard you've all been working on your writing. You are almost ready to read your pieces at our celebration. Today we are going to do something that many writers do. Before we can read our pieces at the author's celebration, we need to make our pieces really beautiful."

Demonstrate how students will do this.

"Today we're going to do this by going back to our pictures and using colored pencils to draw in more the details. This is is a way to make our pieces really beautiful, and also to help the readers of our books understand our stories even more. Watch me do this with my own writing." Leah pulled out her story she planned to publish about a cancelled art class.

The goal for this first cycle of editing is to create the habit, more than to get things right. Leah hopes that as time goes on and children have many opportunities for editing their work, they will become better and better at noticing and correcting their own mistakes. Each time Leah goes through the editing process, she teaches them new strategies for editing.

Leah could have tried to teach a double-decker minilesson, combining this point with her earlier one. But she wisely decided to relegate this second lesson to the Mid-Workshop Teaching Point.

"Remember my cancelled art class story? Well, today I'm going to color in my pictures to make them really beautiful. Let's see—I think the important part of my story was when I cried, so I think I'll color my tears blue right away." She did. "I think I'll also color the trees in all different colors because it was fall. Looking at those trees made me feel better. Do you see what I'm doing? I'm using the colored pencils to put more detail in my pictures and to make them more beautiful and more meaningful. I'm telling you this because you all are going to be doing the same thing in your writing."

Have the students think of how they will add color before they write.

"So, I want you to think about this before you start. I'm going to give you back the beautiful writing pieces you've chosen to publish. First, read your piece to yourself. Then talk to a friend about how you might use the colored pencils today." Leah passed out the children's stories, and there was a quiet hum in the classroom as they read their pieces to themselves. Once Leah saw that the students were done reading and were talking to their friends, she walked around listening to different partnerships discussing what parts of their pictures they might add color to.

Share a few examples before the students go to work on their own.

"Writers, before you get started, listen to what some of your friends are saying they will do today. Talia is going to color in her couch and also color in her cat, because her cat is bright red! She is going to make sure that she colors in her cat the same way on each page. José is going to color in people's faces and color in the slanted eyebrows on his sister's face so that readers know how angry she is in his story."

Send them off to fancy up their work with colored pencils.

"So, writers, for the rest of writing time, let's do what writers do and fancy up our pieces. Work slowly and carefully so that you make your books even more beautiful. Tomorrow is the big day!"

Not all students will pick up on how Leah chooses her colors for reasons related to the content of her story, but some may. This minilesson, like all minilessons, will become multi-level because children will attend to the aspects of the minilesson that make sense to them.

With the plans you choose to share with the whole class, give the children an understanding that they can plan what they will draw and needn't go about it willy-nilly. Some will still do this, of course, and that is to be expected.

Of course, you could have your children use any one of many art supplies to fancy up their work. The main idea is to teach children to work with purpose—in this case, to fancy up their work in some specific way, to some specific end.

TIME TO CONFER

This is your last session in this unit of study and so you'll certainly want to use your conferring checklist to help you think about what your children have and have not learned to do. Pay attention to the big things: their engagement in writing, their understanding of why people write, their abilities and proclivity to work productively with stamina and independence, and their progress as they've moved toward writing coherent detailed texts and toward recording their content using the conventions of written language.

These conferences in *The Conferring Handbook* may be especially helpful today:

▶ *"What's the Story in This Picture?"*
▶ *"Where Is Your Writing?"*
▶ *"Let Me Show You How to Write More"*

Also, if you have *Conferring with Primary Writers*, you may want to refer to the conferences in part one.

After-the-Workshop Share

Invite the children to see what their classmates have done and show their classmates what they have done.

"Writers, today let's leave our work out on the tables and walk around and admire the ways in which we made our writing beautiful."

This is another type of share that we at the Reading and Writing Project call a museum share. Students are given an opportunity to admire one another's work. This share works especially well when you are approaching a publication date because students get to know more intimately what other students are doing.

READING INTO THE CIRCLE: AN AUTHOR'S CELEBRATION

GETTING READY

- Decorations up in the classroom—balloons, a vase of flowers, a tablecloth, a special sign, or even just desks away against the wall
- Juice and cups or a small, special snack— request this of parents or provide it yourself
- Two- or three-line toast— Leah's is at the end of the unit
- See CD-ROM for resources

I WILL NEVER FORGET THE DAY MY FIRST BOOK, Lessons from a Child, *arrived in the mail. I remember hearing the Federal Express truck drive up to the house and thinking, "This is it." I remember tearing the box open and sitting there, my book in my hands, thinking, "I'm an author. I wrote this. My book, by me."*

That single moment utterly changed my life. From that moment on, I have been a writer. My life is infinitely more interesting to me because I'm in the business of spinning it into stories and mining it for insights. More than anything, I want children to learn that they, too, are writers and that they can take the true detail of their lives and put it on the page in ways that will make people gasp and laugh and listen intently and want to hear more. The day that does the most to teach children that they are writers is the day we celebrate children's published work.

There are a few guidelines to follow in planning your celebration. First, remember you'll have at least ten of these across the year—don't make the occasion lavish and exhausting. The celebrations will grow in scale and complexity, so keep this first publication simple. Try to design a celebration that reflects the purposes of the unit. A unit on revision will celebrate drafts. An author study might end with children writing "about the author" pages for their own books.

On this day of the celebration, children will first read into the circle of their classmates, then share their entire piece with a smaller group, and then, after a toast, they'll spend some time drinking juice and talking over the event.

THE CELEBRATION

Make sure the day has a special feel from the moment the children walk into the room by sharing your own excitement.

There was a different feeling in the air on this cool September morning. Students were a bit more dressed up, a bit more excited. "Today's our celebration," Ha said. "I couldn't sleep last night! I was so excited."

"I know," Leah concurred. "It's going to be great! I thought about it the whole time I was exercising in the gym this morning!"

Open the celebration with an air of ceremony and pride in the work the class has done in this unit.

"Writers, let's gather." Leah steeped her voice with excitement. "It's finally time for our celebration." The students came to the meeting area efficiently, as they had practiced, writing in hand and this time they sat in a circle rather than in the ordinary clump. Their writing was in their laps.

The celebration planned on this day is nothing more than a share and a glass of juice, but to the students, the day is bigger than life. Parents or principals aren't invited to this first celebration, although later on they will be. This is the first one. We want it to be intimate and want students to get a sense of how celebrations will go in the classroom.

Leah and I know there can be power in the whole class gathering together and sharing writing; however, we also knows that if we try to have all twenty-five children read their pieces to the class, it will take too long to be celebratory. We decide the whole-class aspect of this celebration will involve each child choosing just his or her favorite page and reading that to the entire class.

Before this day, children practice how this Reading into the Circle will go. They practice forming a circle with their bodies; they have favorite parts of their writing ready and rehearsed. Children learn that when they are finished reading, they must turn to the person on the right so that the next person knows when to begin reading.

"Is this magic?" you may wonder. Twenty-five students come to the meeting area, sit down, and place their writing in their laps? One of the ways you make this day bigger than life is by practicing every part the day beforehand. This practice creates excitement and anticipation and also ensures that the celebration will run smoothly.

"Welcome to 1:102's first writing celebration. I am very proud of all that you have done in writing workshop thus far. You have learned to draw pictures and write words about the things that matter to you. You have also learned that if you get to a hard part, you just do the best you can. You learned how to choose a piece of writing and revise and edit it. You did a great job. You should give yourself a round of applause." They all clapped.

Ask writers to begin Reading into the Circle, and select the student to start the ritual.

"Writers, let's start Reading into the Circle with Casey."

Casey picked up her piece of writing [*Fig. XVII-1*], already open to her favorite page, and read: "And they were twirling around and laughing and telling jokes." Some of the students giggled, remembering the rest of Casey's story.

As she soaked up the giggles, Casey turned her head to the right and looked at Owen. Owen knew this was his signal to start, so he picked up his piece of writing [*Fig. XVII-2*], turned to his favorite page, and read, "Slam down the gooey peanut butter." Everyone giggled again, remembering his recipe for peanut butter sandwiches.

Praise the work children have done that they can do again, in future pieces of writing. Instead of extolling the virtues of the particular pieces they have written, celebrate the processes that are transportable.

And they were twirling around and laughing and telling jokes.

Fig. XVII-1   Casey

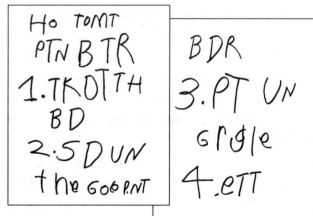

Fig. XVII-2   Owen

How to Make Peanut Butter
1. Take out the bread
2. Slam down the gooey peanut butter
3. Put on Jelly
4. Eat

When Owen looked at her, Alison read just her title page, "Book." Then she turned to her right, to the next reader. This continued until every child in the class had an opportunity to Read into the Circle.

Alison is proud of the title page of her book—she had never made one before and so chose to read that part for her contribution to the celebration.

Leah tries not to say a word from the time the Reading into the Circle starts until the time it ends. This adds to the magic of the ritual and lets the students feel the power of the writing. When there is no talking save for the reading of the words of writers, and the reading goes from one student to the next smoothly, the words can shimmer in the air and students can feel the suspense of waiting for the next reader to begin.

End the Reading into the Circle and begin the process where children share their whole pieces in small groups.

As the last reader finished sharing his or her favorite part, Leah held several beats of silence to allow the words in the air to sink in to the listeners. "Now, with that as the appetizer, we can move to our tables, hear the whole pieces from the people in our groups, and share our own writing! So group one, will you stand up?" On cue, a small group of writers stood up. "You all can read your writing in the back corner. Group two, you may go to the art area. Group three, you may go near the writing center, and group four stay right here."

The children should have practiced the process of moving to their groups, but they may need some reminders about where to meet in the room.

Let the children share their writing and listen to their peers as you walk around to help where needed.

As Leah walked around the room, she stopped occasionally to make sure everyone was listening to the person reading and to solve minor problems, but mostly she was in the background, simply reveling in all that these children had accomplished.

Again, if you didn't know that these youngsters had spent time preparing for this day, it seems nothing short of a miracle.

Bring the reading time to a close and offer a toast to begin the time for refreshments and chatting.

When the reading subsided, it was time for the final phase of the celebration. "Writers, may I have your attention? It looks like most of you have finished reading and are ready to have refreshments. Could you carefully place your lovely writing on the table and come join me at the refreshment table for a quick toast?"

As the students hurried to the table, Leah handed each of them a cup of juice in a brightly colored cup. "You have to wait for the toast," she cautioned as she handed out the juice. "Don't drink it yet."

Once each child had his or her cup of juice, it was time for the toast. "I would like to make a toast (when someone says they are making a toast it means they are about to say some really nice things). Writers, you have worked hard. You deserve this very special day. May we continue to have writing celebrations that are as great as this one. Congratulations!"

The celebration doesn't need to be lavish to feel satisfying to the children. It is the air of importance that you give it that helps children realize the weight of what they have done.

This time for talking after the reading is very important because it helps the little writers to feel that others hear their writing, that it has a real audience in the world.

If Children Need More Time

The purpose of this unit has been to launch your children into a life of writing, and your celebration needs to highlight the fact that each and every child is now an author.

▸ Many teachers make a bulletin board with students after the celebration entitled something like "We Are Writers." This board holds a finished piece of writing from each student next to a photograph of him or her. Some teachers add quotations from children about writing and about themselves as writers. "'I like to write long stories about my grandmother'—Carl" or "'When you think you can't write another word, just get a drink of water and ideas just POP into your head!'—Khadija" or "'When we have writing workshop, we can hear pencils scratching all over the place'—Tally."

▸ You could end the unit by creating a wall with each child having his or her own square to fill. Perhaps each child could bring in artifacts or make pictures that say something about him or her as a writer. Children would then have a chance to talk with each other about what their artifacts and pictures mean about their writing life.

TOURO COLLEGE LIBRARY

3 0000 00144 8251

LB 1576 .C35 2003 v.1
Units of study for primary
  writing
(CD-ROM included)

DATE DUE

LB 1576 .C35 2003 v.1
Units of study for primary
  writing
(CD-ROM included)

AUTHOR

TITLE

DATE DUE	BORROWER'S NAME
2/21/06	Dr. Getman
3/29/07	L. Tehseldar
6-20-07	S. Burton

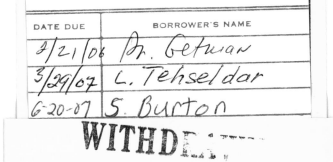

WITHDRAWN

TOURO COLLEGE LIBRARY
Kings Hwy